The Local Politics of Race

Gideon Ben-Tovim
John Gabriel
Ian Law
Kathleen Stredder

MACMILLAN

First published 1986

Published by
MACMILLAN EDUCATION LTD
Houndmills, Basingstoke, Hampshire RG21 2XS
and London
Companies and representatives
throughout the world

Typeset by Acorn Bookwork,
Salisbury, Wiltshire

Printed in Hong Kong

British Library Cataloguing in Publication Data
The local politics of race.—(Public policy and
politics)
1. Associations, institutions, etc.—Great
Britain   2. Great Britain—Race relations
I. Ben-Tovim, Gideon   II. Series
305.8′00941   DA125.A1
ISBN 0–333–37118–6
ISBN 0–333–37119–4 Pbk

Public Policy and Politics

Series Editors: Colin Fudge and Robin Hambleton

Important shifts in the nature of public policy-making are taking place, particularly at the local level. Increasing financial pressures on local government, the struggle to maintain public services, the emergence of new areas of concern, such as employment and economic development, and increasing partisanship in local politics, are all creating new strains but at the same time opening up new possibilities.

The series is designed to provide up-to-date, comprehensive and authoritative analyses of public policy and politics in practice. Public policy involves the expression of explicit or implicit intentions by government which result in specific consequences for different groups within society. It is used by power-holders to control, regulate, influence or change our lives and therefore has to be located within a political context. Two key themes are stressed throughout the series. First, the books link discussion of the substance of policy to the politics of the policy-making process. Second, each volume aims to bridge theory and practice. The books capture the dynamics of public policy-making but, equally important, aim to increase understanding of practice by locating these discussions within differing theoretical perspectives. Given the complexity of the processes and the issues involved, there is a strong emphasis on interdisciplinary approaches.

The series is focused on public policy and politics in contemporary Britain. It embraces not only local and central government activity, but also central–local relations, public-sector/private-sector relations and the role of non-governmental agencies. Comparisons with other advanced societies will form an integral part of appropriate volumes. Each book presents and evaluates practice by drawing on relevant theories and applying them to both the *substance* of policy (for example, housing, employment, local government finance) and to the *processes* of policy development and implementation (for example, planning, management, organisational and political bargaining).

Every effort has been made to make the books in the series as readable and usable as possible. Our hope is that it will be of value to all those interested in public policy and politics – whether as students, practitioners or academics. We shall be satisfied if the series helps in a modest way to improve understanding and debate about public policy and politics in Britain during the 1980s.

Public Policy and Politics

Series Editors: Colin Fudge and Robin Hambleton

Contents

v

Acknowledgements

This book is based on a project which was established in 1978 at Liverpool University and Wolverhampton Polytechnic. We would like to express our thanks to these institutions for their support and in particular for funding two research posts for a three year period, and also to Birmingham Polytechnic and the University of Birmingham for their continuing support. The contents of this book reflect in part the efforts and achievements of many colleagues and friends. In particular we would like to acknowledge staff and members of our two respective Community Relations Councils in Liverpool and Wolverhampton. Our gratitude must also be extended to our families who have been waiting patiently, in some cases with considerable endurance, for the completion of the book; and to Linda Wall, Patricia McMillan and Dianne Murgatroyd for typing the manuscript. Finally we would like to express our gratitude to the Commission For Racial Equality for allowing us to reprint case studies from their annual report and to the Runnymede Trust for allowing us to reproduce material from their monthly bulletin. Ultimately, however, we must take responsibility for the contents of the book.

October 1985

GIDEON BEN-TOVIM
JOHN GABRIEL
IAN LAW
KATHLEEN STREDDER

List of Abbreviations

CRE   Commission For Racial Equality
DES   Department of Education and Science
EMLC   Ethnic Minorities Liaison Committee, Liverpool City Council (a sub-committee of the Housing Allocations Sub-Committee and phased out after the creation of the Race Relations Liaison Committee)
ILEA   Inner London Education Authority
JCC   Joint Consultative Committee
LEA   Local Education Authority
MSC   Manpower Services Commission
MARA Merseyside Anti-Racialist Alliance
MCRC Merseyside Community Relations Council
NUT   National Union of Teachers
RRLC Race Relations Liaison Committee, Liverpool City Council
S11   Section Eleven, Local Government Act, 1966
SCRO Senior Community Relations Officer
WARC Wolverhampton Anti-Racist Committee
WCCR Wolverhampton Council for Community Relations

Guide to Reading the Book

The aim of this book is to provide a framework for analysing local struggles for racial equality. The analysis seeks to establish the role of local institutions in contributing to and maintaining racial inequalities as well as the different kinds of community response to local forms of institutionalised racism. In doing so it explores the nature of the relationship between anti-racist forces and those resistant to positive change, and the integral role of policy initiatives and reforms in helping to define and shape this relationship. Furthermore, it argues that the interests of racial equality are best served through a more direct and organic relationship between research resources on the one hand and political practice on the other. The research data on which this analysis has been developed is drawn from the authors' direct experience of working in local and community organisations in Liverpool and Wolverhampton.

The book is not intended to be used as a textbook or as a guide to further reading. There are many examples of this kind of approach to the field, including a bibliographical essay written by two of the authors (Ben-Tovim and Gabriel, 1979) and more recently a comprehensive bibliography compiled by Gordon and Klug (1984). The references which are cited in the book fall into three categories. The first is made up of secondary sources (i.e. published books and articles) which are used particularly in Chapters 1 and 2 to locate our own position in terms of current debates in race and politics and methods of researching race relations. Secondly there exist a range of primary and secondary sources which we have cited and which help to endorse or substantiate our arguments. In contrast to the first category of reference, the evidence and arguments developed in these sources are crucial to the development of our own analysis. The evidence on racial inequality in Chapter 3 falls into this category. Finally there is a category of primary documents used more directly in the context of our ongoing participation and research based interventions in local politics. Many of the references in Chapters 4, 5 and 6 fall into this category. The bibliography is made up of references cited in the text as a whole.

The first three chapters of the book map out our position in terms of current themes and literature on research (Chapter 1) race and politics (Chapter 2) and racial inequality (Chapter 3). Chapter 4 represents the centre of the book and lies at the heart of our overall project. Its primary focus is local organisations since it has been in local organisations, such as Community Relations Councils and the local Labour Party, that we have drawn our analysis of local authorities (Chapter 5) and central initiatives (Chapter 6). Chapter 4 therefore provides an overview of three different kinds of local organisation concerned with the issue of racial equality: anti-racist, community, and those campaigning for policy change. Although our assessment of Community Relations Councils and local Labour parties is premised on our commitment to these bodies, it is by no means uncritical of their internal functioning and external strategies.

Chapter 5 looks more specifically at the two local authorities in Liverpool and Wolverhampton. Our knowledge and assessment of these has been developed on the basis of our involvement in local campaigns and strategic political interventions. On the one hand we explore various attempts to marginalise anti-racist forces on the part of local politicians and administrators. These in turn have provoked a series of responses on the part of local organisations to counter these pressures and to create power bases from which black people and anti-racist forces can struggle more effectively for racial equality and justice. We assess some of these community based interventions in the second part of Chapter 5.

In Chapter 6 we explore the role of central initiatives, which we have taken to include not only legislation but also government policy documents, circulars and directives as well as reports and statements of national organisations. The significance of these is established again through their impact at the local level and in particular we have witnessed a series of overtly negative measures emanating from the centre that have hindered rather than helped the cause of racial equality. Measures which could be described as positive, in fact, are for the most part the result of the efforts of local organisations. This is because many of the 'positive' initiatives are sufficiently ambiguous and permissive so as to allow a variety of sometimes conflicting local interpretations. Local attempts to realise the limited potential of these measures have been achieved despite rather than because of support from the two local authorities.

The conclusion draws together the threads of our framework. Overall it is intended to provide a basis for reorienting and developing further research in race and possibly other areas of social science as much as it is intended to provide definitive answers to questions. We also hope that it will be used by practitioners and activists (including academics and students) for whom research has seemed remote, largely irrelevant or, worse still, dismissive of their everyday struggles for racial equality.

1 Introduction

The intention of this introductory chapter is to provide an overview of the context in which this book has been conceived and written. In addition to presenting details of the origins and development of the research project, it also identifies both major themes and points of divergence with current traditions within mainstream social science and Marxism. These are discussed particularly with regard to the relationship between research and political practice.

The evolution of the project

This book is an outcome of the research project which we, the four authors, established in 1978. Based in Liverpool and Wolverhampton and supported by Liverpool University and Wolverhampton Polytechnic, the project was conceived during a period of intense political activity on the part of extreme right wing organisations like the National Front. It was also a period during which the anti-racist movement in the form of the Anti-Nazi League and other anti-racist organisations, were attracting wide support. It was not, however, these political forces alone which acted as a catalyst to our project. In fact since the late 1960s there had been a growing concern and involvement – by professional groups (especially those involved in education), by branches of trade unions, by social scientists in academic institutions and even by government (through legislation, reports, etc.) – in the politics of race.

Despite this increasing awareness and take-up of race issues, there was no positive change in the treatment and conditions of black people in Britain. Black children in school remained disadvantaged with those organising and running the educational system seemingly unable to turn recommendations into practice. Black youths and adults became increasingly subject to both unemployment and worsening job conditions, even before the recession advanced and despite the illegality of racial discrimination. The control of black immigration has meant long delay, for those seeking entry into the UK, the separation and splitting up of families and fiancés and the detention of those, including children, suspected of entering this country illegally. It was clear that the 'politics' of racial equality weren't working.

These are issues we refer to in Chapter 2. Our concern here, however, is to point out that it was against the background of mounting evidence of racial inequalities and ineffective political action that we identified the scope and direction of the project. We determined that we would investigate the political process, which we, like many others, saw as a significant force in producing and maintaining inequalities. We obviously also wanted to establish an overview of the political struggle against racism and inequalities.

At the time the project was set up we decided to examine central government policies on race in terms of their impact on local communities, and the scope for local differences in policy and community (including organisational) practice. We intended to pursue this in three stages including first an assessment of central government policies, through interviews with Whitehall officials and the study of policy documents and Hansard. This was to have been followed by a survey of local officials and politicians in Liverpool and Wolverhampton to establish their influence on policy making processes. Finally we were to have assessed the impact of local political and community organisations through interviews with leaders and members but also through active participation. We believed the comparative focus (Liverpool/Wolverhampton) would provide us with an opportunity to establish degrees of difference and variation within a common framework imposed by central government, and to identify sources of local autonomy. Underlying the whole project was a commitment to producing knowledge which would be 'of use' in the struggle for racial equality.

The decision to change the focus and methodology of the project came as a result of a number of obstacles and problems we faced during the first year. The most daunting of these was the refusal of the principal officers in Wolverhampton and Liverpool to give us access to the respective town halls. Effectively this meant that we were deprived of a main source of information – the administrators (or local officers). At the same time our interviews with Whitehall officials (in the Home Office and the Department of the Environment) were proving to be uninformative and inadequate for examining central government's relationship with local authorities, or for building up a detailed knowledge of how race as an issue was 'handled' in Whitehall.

The problems we encountered with central and local government were in direct contrast to our experience of working in and with local organisations. In fact through our involvement in these organisations we found we were gaining a wealth of detail about how local government worked and didn't work. We were also able to study central-local relations on race-related issues and to look at the role of central legislation in promoting racial equality. Of equal importance, we found we were able to use our energy and efforts (for the purpose of research) to support local struggles for racial equality. The nature of our involvement entailed such activities as attending meetings to engage in debates about strategies and objectives; writing policy papers and using them for discussion and lobbying; doing local research for the use of the organisations and attending and organising conferences.

This then was the turning point for the project. We realised that in addition to having access to local organisations, they provided probably the best context for the development of an analysis of the local politics of race. We also realised that if we were serious about taking research out of its ivory tower, this was our chance. Our writing, our discussions, and the development of the analysis would all be carried out in the context of the organisations and would therefore be shared by those committed to racial equality.

By the autumn of 1979, our project had been reformulated. Although the questions which concerned us from the outset of this project remained intact, the means for answering them i.e. the research methods were modified in the light of our experience. Initially we had expected our interviews with Whitehall and the two local authorities to shed light on the nature and impact of central and local policies on racial inequality. Within the framework of our revised methodology, however, we came to assess central and local policies in terms of the problems and possibilities they created for local organisations and local struggles for racial equality. For example this meant that we did not rely on data from the Home Office or Liverpool's chief executive for an understanding of the 1976 Race Relations Act. Rather we came to understand the Act through our active involvement in local anti-racist struggles. In this way our knowledge of central and local policies was linked to the research process through action.

Although we decided to drop the original formal comparative focus (Liverpool and Wolverhampton) we nevertheless felt that our analysis would be strengthened by combining and exchanging our joint experiences and findings. In reality not only has this informed the development of our analysis, but in doing so we would argue it has compounded its validity. In another capacity the Liverpool/Wolverhampton dimension was valuable. Regular meetings of the four researchers provided us with the combination of perspective and focus we needed to return to our respective settings with renewed commitment and confidence.

Finally, it should be noted that our exclusion from local government was a crucial indicator for explaining certain characteristics of the local policy-making process. The result of this was that throughout the remaining five years of the project, the relationship of local government to other local organisations concerned with racial equality, such as the Labour Party and the Community Relations Councils, was consistently tested over a wide spectrum of issues and with us acting in a variety of capacities. We would argue that our findings on this matter are both valid and reliable, and furthermore that they are detailed and specific, as well as explanatory in their content.

In the remainder of this chapter we shall attempt to develop and justify in more detail our method of investigation and analysis. We begin with a brief consideration of two academic traditions within social science both of which have effectively divorced research from political practice.

Politics and research

Ever since the birth of the social sciences in the mid-19th century, there has been continuing controversy surrounding the relationship between the various social scientific disciplines on the one hand and political action on the other. For the past decade or so the conflict has abated giving way to a consensus amongst the major intellectual traditions of the social sciences. By the mid-1980s the effect of this consensus, both within mainstream social science and Marxism, has been to divorce research from political practice.

Mainstream social science is characterised by a confusion over if not a failure to acknowledge the political significance of its research activity. Widespread condemnation of racism and discrimination amongst academics sits uncomfortably alongside a commitment to objectivity in the production and use of research findings. Attempts to depoliticise the research process are unrealisable and serve to undermine attempts to mount a serious and effective challenge to institutionalised racism and inequality. In our view the focus of the research question, the context in which it is carried out and the use to which it is put make the research process political from beginning to end. Social scientists committed to racial equality cannot be satisfied with simply choosing a research topic broadly sympathetic to the aims of anti-racism. Nor can they necessarily expect the results of their research to be taken up by politicians, organisations or local communities in the cause of anti-racism. The tendency to divorce research from its would-be political context and to abstain from research based interventions in politics has only served to sanction the political status quo and in some instances no doubt to actually exacerbate inequalities themselves. Our dispute with much of the sociology of race does not lead us to rule out the possibility of objective research but to try to ensure that the context in which it is carried out is consciously politicised. So long as it is not there will remain a fundamental incompatibility between an ethical stance condemning racism on the one hand and a commitment to objective or apolitical research on the other.

There is a second approach to the study of race relations which, like the first, succeeds in somehow divorcing the writing about and the researching of race from political practice. Ironically, it derives its inspiration from Marxism, a source which in itself might have been expected to have encouraged a more organic relationship between research and political intervention. On the contrary, in our view, much contemporary Marxism has been able to establish a respectable academic niche for itself within the broad disciplinary boundaries of a number of the social sciences. It has been able to do so in the first instance by focusing debate on the ideological purity of Marxism's contemporary forms and their fidelity (or lack of it) to the classical Marxist tradition. Furthermore, this tendency towards academicism (and also sectarianism) is reinforced in a second way through an emphasis on exploring social phenomena in terms of underlying economic and class structures. Variations apart, racism is conceived broadly in terms of capitalist development and the state as an agent of dominant class interests. Nothing short of fundamental restructuring of these determinant factors will significantly reduce racial inequalities or challenge racism. To these ends spontaneous revolt and anti-racist protests are treated as serious forms of political action. On the other hand, activity aimed at reforming existing political structures and introducing institutional and policy change is criticised for concentrating on description at the expense of explanation, for focusing on the surface features of reality such as institutions, policies, reforms and organisations rather than the economic structure which underpins those features and for offering only piecemeal and ineffectual solutions.

In our view however, it is precisely because economic structures on their own yield such poor explanatory returns that we have found it necessary to rely on a more complex analysis of racial inequality. An analysis of the conditions which give rise to inequalities, their institutional mechanisms, the role of central and local policy and the nature of the anti-racist response cannot be considered descriptive, at least not in the terms in which we hope to explore these issues in this book. Nor is the primary purpose of this book to offer solutions, piecemeal or otherwise, on the basis of our analysis. What the book does attempt to do is to explore political action in terms of viable strategic options and to provide a more complex explanation of the limits of reform without preempting it altogether.

The research on which this book is based has sought on the contrary to develop a more integral function for research in the context of political practice. The implications of our attempt to develop this role for research can be spelt out in a number of ways. We can consider its methodological implications more fully and in particular the role of the researcher as practitioner. We can also look at it from the other side, from the standpoint of the practitioner as researcher. In terms of the first of these it would be appropriate at this stage to consider a research tradition which has gone some way to confronting and resolving a number of the problems identified above. The tradition has become known as action research.

Action research

Action research is a well estabished if unfashionable tradition in the social sciences which has a long track record in the field of industrial organisations and in the work of the Tavistock Institute in particular, but which has more recently become associated with initiatives designed to combat the effects of urban deprivation and disadvantage. The most significant of these have included the War on Poverty Programmes in the United States and the Education Priority Areas and Community Development Projects in the United Kingdom in the late 1960s and early 1970s.

Although the above examples of action research sought to develop action programmes on the basis of research evidence, one of their most enduring problems arose from the distinction which was made between action and research and the corresponding division of responsibilities between those who researched and those who acted. (See for example Lees and Smith, 1975.) One consequence of this separation, of particular concern to us, has been the frequent failure of action research to take account of its political context and the implications of its chosen programme of action. Such difficulties could be overcome, in our view, through the abandonment of any formal division of action and research responsibilities. The absence of any form of institutional differentiation between the research or research team and the activist or action team brings about a role fusion which we have sought to develop in our work in Liverpool and Wolverhampton.

The unity of research and action has three consequences which are important to note. The first has to do with the relationship between policy and research, and the use to which research is put. The policies of central and local government, private firms, nationalised industries, trade unions, schools and local organisations all serve to define and limit inequalities within social relations. For those actively engaged in political struggle for racial equality, policies help to structure the conditions and terms of that struggle. To ignore or dismiss them is to ignore the means for further advance. Policy analysis thus provides a necessary pre-condition for coherent research practice, that is to say for research which is developed consistently in terms of an initial commitment to racial equality. The policy implications of research cannot there-fore be relegated to the status of an after-thought, or to a set of recommendations made in a political vacuum. Rather the implica-tions of research become an object of investigation in their own right, and an analysis of the means by which they might be implemented or used become an integral part of the research pro-cess itself, built in from the outset.

In the second place the integration of research and action requires researchers to develop direct links with organisations con-cerned with political change, from campaigning bodies to those statutory agencies responsible for policy implementation. Research is thus developed out of some kind of organisational base. What is more, effective research-based interventions require a full analysis of the organisations or agencies themselves in terms of their objectives, strategies and organisational structures. The purpose of this form of internal evaluation is to contribute directly to the effectiveness of these bodies in realising their external polit-ical and policy objectives. Overall, both these consequences of breaking with the action-research distinction entail a commitment to inject the products of social science into the political and policy process. These injections take a variety of different forms and are made at a number of levels, a reflection of the complexity of the process by which political decisions and policy implementation actually occur. (See, for example, Cherns, 1979.)

Finally the assimilation of research and practice is reflected in the status of the knowledge produced as a result of this process. Whatever the merits of large scale surveys, say of local authority policies, or even in depth interviews, say with community leaders, the results of these kinds of research methods are always limited. Their implications arise from the nature of the relationship bet-ween researcher and what or who is being researched which in the above examples will vary but will always be relatively superficial, external and ephemeral. This must in turn be reflected in the nature as well as the reliability of the responses to survey questions which form the basis of subsequent interpretation and analysis. In contrast there is a kind of knowledge which can be constructed out of political practice, for which there is no substitute. It demands a continuous interplay of calculation and testing through struggle within a political context. Questions asked can be tested against past performance and if necessary asked again. Policy statements can be measured in terms of their impact over time, as well as influenced directly through collaborative political intervention. Organisations can be understood not just in terms of their constitutions or on the basis of selective and guarded statements of their leaders but through direct and sustained involvement over relatively long periods of time.

To summarise, previous action-research projects have had the effect of legitimising the role of action in research practice, and they have also effectively challenged the notion of apolitical, or value-free, research. Our model of action-research has adopted these principles, but has acknowledged the fact that for these to increase the potential impact of research on political analysis and policy, they must be realised through the integration of research and action. In effect this means that research must acknowledge its political connections, in terms of its explicit aims, the realities of the context it has chosen to research and the implications of these for political intervention including policy implementation. Race relations research which appears ostensibly committed to anti-racism or the elimination of racial discrimination but which is not explicitly designed to effect any change in those directions, effectively serves to maintain if not to endorse the status quo and sometimes, albeit unwittingly, to legitimate further inequalities.

Research and political activity: the citizen as social scientist

Our attempt to break from research which isolates itself from political practice has been looked at so far from the point of view of the 'researcher'. But it also follows from what has been argued so far that other groups of workers and volunteers including professionals, individual trade unionists and activists working in the community including black organisations will be strategically placed to develop alternative forms of research-based interventions to those

analysed in this book. These groups will have access to different
kinds of knowledge, and hence be involved in different forms of
political, sometimes policy intervention.

In saying this, we do not wish, nor are we in a position to argue
for the superiority of any one particular mode of research-based
intervention. Rather our argument is compatible with a wide but
complementary range of anti-racist activities. The variety of different forms will reflect the range of positions and contexts from
which anti-racist activities can be developed, as well as the varying
contributions that any individual can most usefully make to that
struggle. We would therefore strongly resist attempts to give priority to one form of intervention to the exclusion of other forms of
activity. In our view, the sectarian claim that only one form of
anti-racist activity is authentic, for example activity on the streets,
or by black people alone, has been a source of considerable confusion and division within the anti-racist movement.

The separation of action and research has encouraged a squan-
dering of potentially useful resources and militated against the
construction of significant alliances. On the one hand universities
and other academic institutions control a range of useful resources
which, if directly harnessed to anti-racist struggle, could provide a
valuable influx of skill and resources. On the other hand, the bad
reputation of 'research', together with misconceptions about its
potential, has meant that political activists and organisations have
frequently failed to build a research function into their operation.
In our view 'research' should be seen as a normal attribute of
political action which involves, or should involve, a form of
analysis based on a realistic and concrete assessment of the balance
of political forces and the consequences of different courses of
action.

Action research then is not only for academic social scientists
(both black and white) but also for individuals and groups committed to anti-racism. In both cases, we would submit, this research
involves, in general terms, identifying the specific forms of injustice and inequality and their institutional sources, and then
developing strategies for building support and weakening resistance. Thus casework social workers may be able to mobilise support for changes in policy and practice on the basis of their contact
with, and knowledge of the grievances of, their black clients. Community Relations Officers may compile dossiers of incidents of

racial harassment on council estates and use them to criticise and campaign for changes in the policies and local practices of housing departments. Labour Party activists may attempt to change local party policy on ethnic monitoring on the basis of information gathered from other Labour parties in different localities and from national Labour Party policy documents. Finally black womens' organisations may organise surveys to find out problems faced by black women in their experiences of ante-natal provision within the National Health Service and use these as a basis for articulating campaign demands at strategic points in the political process.

The above random examples indicate the variety of contexts and institutions and the range of workers and volunteers potentially able to perform a research function within their institutions. On the other hand the research resources of our educational and research institutions, particularly those devoted to race relations, should acknowledge the political dimension to their research activity. By aiming their analyses at political intervention and therefore at the contexts in which struggles are 'lost' and 'won', they would not only contribute to the development of those struggles, but they would also produce an analytical framework and a substantive knowledge that would reflect the political complexity and dynamic of the field.

In this chapter we have attempted to locate the arguments developed in this book in terms of its research context. We have done so in particular through an attempt to develop a process of research which acknowledges its inseparability from politics. In the next chapter we develop our position more precisely with reference to current literature and themes surrounding the politics of race.

2 The Politics of Race: Current Themes and Issues

This chapter will attempt to develop a rationale for the book as a whole, beyond the issues raised in the Introduction. It will do so via a discussion of some of the current themes and issues surrounding the politics of race as they have been developed in the literature. With this we shall attempt to offer further clarification to our own position which in general terms represents an attempt to integrate two positions which invariably run in parallel if not in divergent directions from one another.

The first of these positions is well illustrated in E. J. B. Rose's book *Colour and Citizenship*. Published in 1969, its intention was to look at the response of government and local services to the arrival and presence of black minority groups in Britain. It concluded that racial discrimination was a common experience of black immigrants seeking employment and housing, and it argued the case for the dispersal of minority groups and the strengthening of anti-discrimination legislation and anti-poverty programmes. The emphasis of this analysis on social policy was unfashionable at the time, but worse still in the eyes of its critics, it was guilty of identifying the immigrant as the problem and ignoring the wider socio-economic structure (Zubaida, 1970).

Almost as if in reaction, the research and political analysis characteristic of the 70s turned to focus on class, immigration, racism and the role of successive governments. In particular there was a concern to demonstrate that racism was a function of capitalism through establishing that immigration legislation was above all a response to the needs of a capitalist economy and that the creation of a black 'underclass', 'fraction', 'reserve army', or 'sub-

12

proletariat' was thus inevitable. This hypothesis, considered along-side Parliament's record on immigration, implicated both the Labour and Conservative parties and in so doing removed the possibility for discussing policy options and alternatives. The politics of race was thus removed from the policy arena (that is, the political issue was not seen to be linked to any form of positive directed change), except for the narrow debate about whether or not Britain should have immigration legislation. The political analysis which highlights racism as a function of capitalism has continued to be very popular at least insofar as it dictates a starting point and framework for posing problems and questions.

Despite this emphasis on racism and immigration as class politics during the 1970s, research studies of policy continued to be published. Some, most notably the PEP (Daniel, 1968; Smith, 1977) and PSI (Brown, 1984) studies have documented the wide-spread existence of racial inequalities. Others have been aimed at particular areas of policy and service provision (for example the main body of the Scarman Report (1981) and the PSI report (1983) both focusing on the police and Little and Willey (1981) on educational policy and race). More recently others have been more concerned with policy implementation, for example Young and Connelly (1980) whose study provides a detailed report of equal opportunity and multiracial policies in six local authorities.

In general terms, therefore, the politics of race has developed two approaches: one concerned with the politics of immigration and racism in terms of class structure, and another whose explicit focus has been policy issues. As a result of this compartmentalisation within the literature, political analysis has often lacked a policy dimension, whilst policy issues have invariably been divorced from their political context.

In order to facilitate the integration of these two areas, policy analysis must confront two significant and challenging political problems. Firstly policy analysis needs to accommodate the notions of anti-racist and black struggles. The majority of policy studies are aimed at specifying the content of the required reform, or the technical means by which the reform will be implemented, rather than *how* the reform will be achieved, or how its overall objective, for example equality or justice, will be monitored and maintained. Without making reference to grassroots struggle these omissions are not surprising. On the other hand, their inclusion could make a substantial contribution to both the content and method of change.

Another significant problem is that of undertaking an analysis of policy which recognises that policy is an instrument of change and therefore requires an evaluation in light of its potential. Although there is ample evidence that existing legislation and policy have so far made very little impact on reducing racial inequalities, there is every indication that they could both be developed and used more effectively for this purpose. The fact that legislation and policy legitimate and frame the principles and the practice of institutional racism is further reason for serious critical analysis. Finally recognising policy as an instrument of change means acknowledging the responsibilities of our political institutions and organisations, and those chosen to represent and take up these issues. The link between inadequate or bad policy and the realities of our political system are rarely traced.

The aim of this chapter is thus to locate our own position, developed in the book as a whole, through a critical examination of current trends in the literature on political and policy issues in race. Overall what we seek to do in both our analysis of racial inequality and political attempts to eliminate it is to broaden the scope of both policy and political analysis in an effort to integrate the strengths of the literature representing both traditions.

The politics of racial inequality

The emphasis in political analyses of race has focused on the role of successive post-war governments in institutionalising racism particularly through their policies on immigration. Commentaries have thus stressed the part played by legislation and policies both in controlling the numbers of immigrants of Afro-Caribbean and Asian descent, and in curtailing and controlling the rights and activities of those black people already settled in the UK. Both sets of legislative and policy measures have become regarded as the principal political mechanisms through which racial inequalities are generated, reproduced and sanctioned. The ideological rationale underpinning immigration legislation and control is couched in terms of an array of social and economic problems which, it is alleged, arise directly as a result of black immigration. What we shall argue below is that discussions of racism in these terms have tended to restrict themselves to a somewhat narrow range of policies which in turn are held to be rationalised in terms of a narrow conception of racist ideology.

Racism, politics and immigration

Formal legal control of immigration from the New Commonwealth began in 1962. The successful passing of the Act of that year, itself a volte-face from previous policy, has been associated with a number of historical factors: mounting grassroots pressure from within the ranks of the Conservative party, perhaps the best known example of which was Cyril Osborne's Immigration Control Association; fears, articulated inside Parliament, of more violence of the kind witnessed in the street disturbances of Notting Hill and Nottingham in the late 1950s; unemployment, increasing in the aftermath of the period of post-war reconstruction and finally perceived pressures on public services, including health, housing and education, attributed to the influx of New Commonwealth immigrants in the 1950s. The Commonwealth Immigrants Act of 1962 is deemed significant not only because it was the first legal attempt to limit the numbers of what to all intents and purposes were black people from entering the UK. Black can be used here as a generic term describing those of Afro-Caribbean and Asian descent who were being linked effectively as political subjects through legislation.

More significant perhaps was the political spirit in which it was passed, a case of the 'racist tail wagging the parliamentary dog' as one author has described this period (Fryer, 1984, p. 381). In other words it made official the view that violence, unemployment and deteriorating public services had something to do with the presence of black immigrants. In brief, the Act restricted immigration from the New Commonwealth to those with jobs to come to (Category A) or with skills to offer (Category B) and placed a ceiling on a third category (C) of would-be unskilled labour.

The 1962 Act was followed by a series of legislative and policy measures introduced by both Conservative and Labour governments. The 1965 White Paper *Immigration from the Commonwealth* (Home Office, 1965) gained its notoriety because it brought the official view of the Labour party into line with Conservative party policy by extending the restrictions on immigration introduced in the 1962 Act, namely that social problems such as housing and unemployment can indeed be ameliorated through immigration control. According to Sivanandan, the White Paper took discrimination out of the market place and gave it the sanction of the state. It made racism respectable and clinical by institutionalising it (1982, p. 109).

Other measures followed, each with its own particular claim to notoriety. The significance of the Labour government's Commonwealth Immigrants Act 1968 lies both in the circumstances in which it was passed and in the legal loophole it created which permitted white Britons from Kenya to slip through the net of immigration control. The Act was designed to restrict entry of British passport holders from Kenya who, following a ruling by the Kenyan government, were no longer guaranteed rights of settlement in that country. At the time of Kenyan Independence in 1963 nationals were allowed to opt for Kenyan citizenship or to retain their British (Commonwealth) citizenship. It was this latter group who were affected by the ruling of the Kenyan government. Undoubtedly fear of a further influx of black immigrants provoked the Labour government to respond swiftly. As a result of the 1968 Act, Kenyans with British passports were to be treated like any other New Commonwealth citizen and hence were subject to the same entry restrictions. The prospect of creating a stateless category of black British Kenyans was thus ultimately agreed to by the British government. However, there were also a group of white expatriates settled in Kenya who had remained there after independence. Their rights of entry to and settlement in the UK were secured through the legal loophole, patriality, in the 1968 Act, which made an exception of those whose father or grandfather had acquired British citizenship by birth, naturalisation and registration. It was the first but by no means the last time this discriminatory device was involved in immigration (and nationality) law.

The most recent immigration law, passed in 1971, did indeed extend the notion of patriality to cover all those from the New Commonwealth with 'special family ties' to the UK. For the remainder, entry was to be based on 12-monthly work permits which need or need not be renewed at the discretion of the Home Secretary and his interpretation of 'good behaviour'. Sivanandan attempted to encapsulate the shifts in post-war immigration policy in the title of one of his many articles on this issue, 'From Immigration Control to Induced Repatriation' (Sivanandan, 1982) and elsewhere with reference to the shift from Commonwealth immigration to migrant labour.

Those civil servants and ministers involved in drawing up the detailed provisions of the 1981 British Nationality Act, were thus in a position to establish who was and who was not a British citizen and what rights were to accompany this status. In doing so they were required to work through the already complex legal status arising from colonisation, independence and of course the desire to bring nationality into line with immigration law in order to sanction existing discriminatory provisions. The latter was achieved by distinguishing British from British Overseas Citizenship and linking the first once more to the notion of 'close connection' with the UK or patriality.

Moreover the effects of policies on immigration and nationality are not confined to the racially discriminatory laws themselves. The Immigration Act and the immigration rules have been policed and administered with considerable force and effectiveness, at least according to evidence documented by the Runnymede Trust (1984) and by the CRE (1985).

The Nationality Act too has had its wider ramifications. Recent changes in law and rules governing access to health, education and social security have made citizenship the basis for eligibility to these public services. Proof of citizenship can be required at the discretion of the official which often means that those seemingly least likely to quality or rather those who are more physically identifiable are singled out for checking purposes (Manchester Law Centre).

Racism, politics and ideology

In a radio interview in 1978, Margaret Thatcher spoke of the need to end immigration in order to avoid the effects of being 'swamped' by an alien culture (cited in Barker, 1981, p. 15). At the same time, and in order to justify her otherwise ethnocentric and racist remark, Mrs Thatcher made reference to Britain's contribution to democracy and freedom throughout the world.

In terms of its repercussions, Mrs Thatcher's comment relied heavily on the by then well-established popular misconception that Britain had been and still was being 'taken over by black immigrants'. It was this idea that had first fuelled general election issues in the 1960s and which had been used to arouse popular support for the introduction of immigration legislation throughout this period. The irony in terms of Mrs Thatcher's intervention was that primary immigration from the New Commonwealth, excluding dependants and relatives with a legitimate right to enter to be with those already settled in the UK, had already effectively been brought to a standstill by the 1971 Act. A further irony was that the Act itself, with its patriality provision, and the UK's subsequent accession to the EEC, conferred a legal right of entry on many millions of immigrants, the vast majority of whom, of course, were white. Nevertheless Mrs Thatcher's comments undoubtedly provided one rationale for subsequent tightening up in the rules governing the administration of immigration in 1981, as well as helping to create a political atmosphere conducive to her own forthcoming electoral success.

More significantly perhaps, Mrs Thatcher's view has been interpreted as reinforcing new popular images of racism, for instance those associating young black people with street crime. Examples of these new forms of racist ideology have been cited by Stuart Hall in his research into the media in the 1970s (Hall *et al.*, 1978). In particular Hall revealed the growth of and interest in media coverage of young blacks involved in 'mugging'. Mugging thus became one of the social phenomena of the 1970s, and one identified with the activities of young blacks. Young blacks thus became an integral focus of the law and order campaign on which the Conservative party fought the general election of 1979. At least one commentator has suggested the decline in electoral fortunes of the National Front in the late 1970s can be attributed in part to the issues on which the Conservative Party fought the 1979 general election (Edgar, 1977). The Conservative's high profile stance on both immigration and law and order served to undermine the potential distinctiveness of the National Front's campaign.

Young black people thus joined the celebrated ranks of a series of 'social misfits' held to be (somewhat ambiguously) both responsible for and symptomatic of Britain's post-war economic decline and moral demise. Militant trade unionists, progressive teachers, revolutionary students, the work-shy unemployed as well as immigrants have all at some point in post-war history fallen prey to popular attack. This in turn has been used to justify some political response, ranging from industrial relations legislation, the creation and expansion of the Manpower Services Commission, changes in social security legislation and administration or increased immigration control.

How these links are forged between public attitudes, political debate and policy interaction, and why the 'creation' of these problem groups appears almost inevitable, have all been the subject of more general debate. The concept of ideology has been used to disentangle some of these problems, although it has yet to provide answers to all of the above questions, if indeed it can. In an article concerned with ideologies of race and the media, Stuart Hall (1981) makes use of a particular conception of ideology which attempts to break with the constraining effects of past attempts to conceptualise the term. Ideologies, Hall says, represent explanations (or chains of meaning) of the way things are. For instance they may serve to explain why there is a shortage of public housing in terms of the presence of immigrant groups, or to explain the increase in street crime in terms of the presence of young black people. Ideologies which provide these readily intelligible, plausible accounts of social reality, provide us with the means to think about the world. We do not choose one ideology against another. The processes by which one is used and not another are complex but are not reducible to an act of free will. In Hall's research the media and the tabloid press reinforced, if not helped to create, these links between moral decay, social crisis and a particular portrayal of young blacks, with their rastafarian dreadlocks, reggae music and ganja.

In terms of Stuart Hall's analysis, therefore, a popular consensus emerged during the 1970s which provided us with the means to understand and explain the so-called riots of 1980 in St Pauls in Bristol and in 1981 in Brixton, Liverpool 8, Southall, Moss Side and many other British towns and cities. The links between street crime, indiscipline in the home, falling educational standards, decline in moral values, and young black people had already found a place in popular thinking. What is more, politicians seized on them in their own versions of events of that period. Mark Carlisle, then Secretary of State for Education, identified the real underlying factor to be 'a breakdown in the stabilising forces of society: the nation, patriotism, the family and the whole community (*The Times*, 18.7.81). William Whitelaw too considered the relative absence of parental control to be a major factor whilst others made reference to individual wickedness and hooliganism (Kettle and Hodges, 1982, Ch. 7).

These interpretations of the conflicts of the early 1980s, at one level can and have been used to sanction police demands for extending their powers of search, arrest and detention in order to combat the 'problem'. (Lord Scarman, for instance, in his official enquiry into the Brixton disorders, supported proposals for strengthening police powers, although it must be said this ran alongside a series of 'softer' proposals which we shall consider shortly). A number of the provisions in the Police and Criminal Evidence Act are intended to either extend or sanction existing police powers. As far as young black people are concerned, it is not so much that the Act is explicitly discriminatory. Its implementation however will undoubtedly lead to an even greater number of searches, arrests, detentions, court appearances, custodial sentences for young blacks than current figures which anyway already indicate an imbalance (Gordon, 1984, Ch. 5). Like so much current public policy, it is the interpretation and application of the law in the context of a particular understanding of the problems, one, moreover which has been officially sanctioned repeatedly in post-war political history, which is likely to reinforce and increase existing racial inequalities in the legal system.

Broadening the analysis of racism and the politics of racial inequality

From the discussion so far it is clear that existing literature attaches considerable significance to the role of successive post-war governments in contributing to and sanctioning racial inequalities. Both major political parties have done so principally through the introduction and extension of legislation controlling immigration from the New Commonwealth. The significance of these controls lies not just in their day to day impact on would be immigrants and their families. Nor does it just lie in the patriality provisions *per se*, constituting as they do a most explicit form of indirect racial discrimination. Their significance lies as much in the rationale underpinning legislation, which serves to endorse the claim that a variety of social ills are attributable to the presence of immigrants and their descendents. The corollary of this in policy terms has implied greater control over black people already settled here. Recent attempts to regulate access to social security, health and education provision following the Nationality Act and to extend police powers in these situations in which young blacks find themselves, in disproportionate terms, brought into contact with the police, are all examples of the exercise of this control. Politics through governments and their bureaucracies have not only sanctioned inequality; they have made it part of the day to day exercise of political power. In other words the creation and perpetuation of racial inequality has been institutionalised through politics.

Our own research although more directly concerned with local government and politics, confirms both in general and in detail the negative impact of the underlying ideology and day-to-day reality of immigration and other legislation, such as the Police and Criminal Evidence Act. In fact in both Liverpool and Wolverhampton much of our on-going action research was committed to taking up these issues through our involvement in local organisations.

We would not, however, wish to restrict analysis of the state to the role of post-war governments, and state racism to policies on immigration and the police. The overly narrow focus, evident in much of the literature, encourages, in our view, an analysis of immigration and related political responses which fails to take account of the deeply embedded nature of institutional racism. This is not to deny that the race issue has certainly become popularised through media scares about Malawians in four star hotels, the immigration and repatriation debates assisted by Enoch Powell, the debate surrounding 'black mugging', popular interpretations of 'riots' and their policy implications (for example the strengthening of police powers and severer sentences for those convicted). Nevertheless to remain at the level of racism's most overt and popularised manifestations is to some extent to detract from a variety of forms of racism which operate through equally complex political processes. The former make up the blunt end of forces for racial inequality. The latter, although less obvious and recognisable in terms of their immediate impact, have a permanence and a durability which is equally devastating in its effects. It is racism's low profile which we would wish to draw attention to, not only for the purpose of uncovering further layers of institutional racism, but also for the contribution it can make to our understanding of the politics of race and racism.

In this book we identify not one, but several forms of institutionalised racism. We use the term racism to refer to a process the outcome of which is racial inequality. In this sense therefore we identify a variety of processes through which racism operates: laws, policies, administrative practice, all of which can discriminate directly (that is overtly designed or intentionally discriminatory) or indirectly (that is discriminatory in terms of their effects). Consequently the ideologies or explanations or rationales for such processes are by no means reducible to an equation which links the numbers of immigrants to social problems. For example, Militant leaders of Liverpool's City Council effectively discriminate not because they are operating with the idea that Liverpool is being swamped by black immigrants or that Liverpool's black population equals a local problem. On the contrary certain brands of socialism have their own ideologies which in terms of their effects also perpetrate existing racial inequalities. They do so through a refusal to acknowledge the specific forms of institutionalised racism *vis-à-vis* other processes which give rise to class inequalities. In this sense we would argue there can be two levels at which racism operates: at the level of policies, rules or their interpretation, and at another level in the refusal to acknowledge racism and/or do something about it.

Similarly universalism in policy making which supports the view that everyone should be treated equally, irrespective of already existing inequalities, can and does serve to maintain existing racial inequalities. Once again the specific problem of racism is subsumed to a broader set of values, so that like militant socialism, liberal universalism reinforces racial inequalities in ways which can be identified through an analysis of political processes.

The above ideologies, although significant, by no means exhaust available chains of meaning or understandings of race problems and their solutions. Nor do we pretend that our analysis in this book exhausts all possibilities. Its focus is local and our evidence in the main comes from two geographical areas and is limited in terms of the political processes and policy areas with which we have some experience. Nevertheless it can serve to strengthen arguments for a more detailed examination of racism and political processes than those currently discussed within the field of the politics of race.

In addition to the tendency in the literature to emphasise one of racism's many ideological forms, there is a second sense in which current analyses have served to restrict the focus of debate: in particular through a tendency to confine politics to governments (Labour and Conservative) and the state to the more overtly coercive of its institutions such as the police.

In attempting to broaden both politics and the state we shall use the latter to refer to three interrelated sets of political forms and processes. In the first place we shall use it to refer to a set of public institutions, including central, regional and local government and their respective administrations. They are public in the sense that *at some point* there exists political representation, which is ultimately answerable or accountable to an electorale. We stress at some point since the relationship between electoral constituencies, representatives and public institutions is by no means a straightforward one. As a result some are considerably more public than others. Secondly we shall refer to the state in terms of its relationship with institutions outside the formal apparatus of representative democracy. This relationship can be explored in terms of the way public bodies regulate and provide a framework for activity outside their domain, again through laws, policies and administrative practices. Laws regarding monogamous marriages, tax and social security legislation regarding the status of dependents and prescriptions regarding domestic arrangements, as well as race relations law which relates to treatment of and provision for racial minorities, are all examples of how the state regulates activities outside its own formal boundaries. Finally we shall refer to the state as a site of struggles where the object is to change the role of public institutions in terms of their status and/or their relationship to bodies outside their formal institutional boundaries.

Our understanding of these struggles in terms of their participants, who or what the struggle is aimed at, the conditions within which it is being waged and an assessment of its effects requires a full analysis of the state in all three cases. It is then possible to indicate how struggles themselves can serve to redefine the boundaries of the state and its internal/external relations. This brings us back to the argument that there is a need to broaden the conception of politics and the state in order to grasp the complex forms

and processes which help to structure and define racial inequalities. Were it not for the presence of political forces working
against racism and for racial equality the inequalities could be all
the more marked. In order to broaden our conception of politics
still further therefore we need to consider in general terms those
political forces working in support, or appearing in support, of
racial equality.

Policy, politics and the struggle for racial equality

By way of contrast, there is much less of a literature on the politics
of reducing racial inequality. What has been written may be
broken down into three areas. In the first instance there has been a
tendency to focus on attempts of both black and white organisations and groups to combat racism's most overt and extreme manifestations, ranging across immigration control, racial attacks, the
activities of the far right and policing. Much less has been written
in more explicit terms on black politics either in terms of participation in mainstream political parties or single issue campaigns. Nor
has much been written about black organisations themselves
although this does relate to an area which has received limited
coverage, namely the role of black workers in industrial disputes.
Finally as far as official policy responses to racial inequality is
concerned there has been a tendency to focus, generally somewhat
dismissively, on three government initiatives on race relations and
inner city deprivation. On this basis it is clear that there is a need to
develop a much fuller and more comprehensive analysis of political forces engaged in struggles for racial equality. For this analysis
to be purposeful, however, it would need to be developed in the
context of a more politically conscious form of research practice.
(We have referred to what this might be in the Introduction.)

Once again in locating our own position we shall retrace the
steps of others. In doing so we shall find that answers to the questions of what is, and what can be done, to combat racial inequality
are rarely given the full treatment they deserve.

Anti-racist and black struggles

We have restricted our historical focus in this chapter to the post-
war period, although it is important to acknowledge that resistance

to racial harassment, racial attacks, and street conflicts involving the police and the black community, is not a peculiarly post-war phenomenon. The best documented of these are the conflicts which took place in the cities of Cardiff and Liverpool in particular following demobilisation at the end of World War I. Numerous incidents of attacks and racial abuse provoked situations in which black people were not only defending themselves against 'lynch mobs' but also the police. Many injuries resulted and some deaths, one of the best known of which is probably that of a young black seaman, Charles Wootton in Liverpool in 1919 (Fryer, 1984, p. 300). Again in 1948, black seamen in Liverpool defended themselves against racial abuse and assault. As before, this resulted in a concentration of police resources on the black community, and in the ensuing street conflicts and arrests many eyewitness accounts were reported of police violence, of beatings and serious injuries received by members of the black community (Fryer, 1984, p. 367).

In the post-war period these traditions (for both harassment and resistance) have continued. The street conflicts of Nottingham and Notting Hill in the late 1950s have been considered in terms of a similar set of factors, that is to say, a background of intimidation ('nigger-hunting lynch mobs'), assault, the operation of 'colour bars' and, in the case of Notting Hill, the activities of fringe right wing organisations. The police response to such overt hostility and discrimination was not merely indifferent but hostile and aggressive to the black community, particularly insofar as sections of that community sought to defend themselves against further attack.

The emergence of anti-fascist, anti-racist organisations in the 1970s must be set against this background, of which the above cited examples were by no means isolated. The most successful and certainly the best known of these organisations was the Anti-Nazi League which was launched in 1977. Its emergence clearly coincided with the electoral achievements of the National Front, by far Britain's most successful post-war fascist organisation. On a national basis the ANL waged a successful propaganda war drawing popular support for anti-fascism through the associations drawn between past and present fascist organisations. At a local level, the ANL and anti-racist committees similarly sought to prevent the escalation of fascist activity often through attempts to prevent marches or meetings from being held (a 'no platform' stance) and failing that, the organisation of counter marches, demonstrations and leafleting. Beyond their opposition to these, the activities of the NF and other such organisations, local anti-racist committees have tended to concentrate their efforts on combating particular forms of institutional racism particularly with regard to policing and immigration issues. During this period numerous cases of racial attacks, police harassment including deaths in police custody and deportation were brought to the attention of these committees. Some became national issues, if not in the mainstream media, at least in the socialist and black press for example the cases of: the Mangrove Nina following a police raid on a London restaurant in 1971; David Oluwale, involving an alleged death in police custody in 1971; Gurdip Chagger, who was stabbed to death by white youths in Southall in 1976; Blair Peach who died on an anti-National Front demonstration in Southall during which the police clashed with demonstrators and Anwar Ditta, Nasira Begum and Mohammed Idrish, three cases of deportation in 1983–4.

Cases of this kind have provided significant issues around which black communities have organised themselves politically. A number of the black youth organisations and movements which emerged in the 1970s, in Southall, Brick Lane, Leicester, Manchester and Bradford, followed individual cases of murder within their communities (Sivanandan, 1982, p. 142). The celebrated court cases of the Bradford Twelve and Newham Eight are both linked to attempts on the part of the black community to defend themselves in response to continuous harassment by sections of the white community including the police.

Struggles against racism have not, however, been confined to the street. At work black people have fought to establish trade union recognition for parity of pay, and for opportunities to exercise their rights within the trade union movement. Examples have included the struggles at Mansfield Hosiery Mills, for high wages and against job reservation for whites; Imperial Typewriters, which highlighted problems with the union as well as conditions of work including wages and Grunwick, where union recognition was the issue most prominently highlighted. There have been many others, a number of which have been documented over the years in *Race Today*, *The Black Liberator*, *Race and Class*, *Bradford Black* and other newspapers and journals produced by the black community in Britain.

The emergence of black women's organisations in the 1970s, must in part be linked to their leading role in a number of the above industrial struggles (including for example Imperial Typewriters and Grunwick) and immigration cases (for example Ditta and Begum). It must also be linked to broader developments within feminist politics during that decade. Apart from the above issues of concern to all black people living in Britain black women's groups focused on issues of particular concern to women including: social security with reference to child benefits, urgent needs benefits; health, for example the campaign on Depro Provera and immigration particularly concerned with the rights and status of fiancées, dependent relatives and the problems arising from extended leave. Both Asian and Afro-Caribbean groups formed an umbrella body OWAAD (Organisation of Women of Afro-Caribbean and Asian Descent) in 1978. Local groups continue to emerge. Some are more pan-Africanist and internationalist in their perspective, whilst others have an orientation towards domestic policy. Some receive grant aid through central and local government funding whilst others resist state aid as a matter of principle. Although a number run their own bulletins and newspapers, very little has been documented in books and articles on black women's politics.

Although its record on race is hardly unblemished, the Labour Party continues to be viewed by the majority of black voters in Britain as the most likely party for positive change. This can be explained in part in terms of Labour's appeal to a predominantly black working class constituency and its record on race relations initiatives. All three Race Relations Acts have been passed by Labour governments in contrast to the Conservative party who are much more closely associated with immigration control and Powellism. Neither of these factors however can guarantee continuing support for Labour. There are signs of frustration with the relative lack of representation within the Labour Party. There are no black MPs, a relatively small and moreover concentrated number of black councillors and a relatively small active black membership within the Party. Attempts to ensure some minimum representation are currently being made in the demand for the establishment of black sections within the Party, analogous to women's sections. The issue became the subject of a National Executive Committee (of the Labour Party) working party enquiry, and an agenda item at successive Labour Party conferences. There is evidence too of a Conservative vote within the Asian community particularly within its entrepreneurial class (Anwar, 1980), so that developments within the Labour Party and changing perceptions of interest linked to affiliation are factors which will affect the nature and form of black participation in mainstream politics in the future (Fitzgerald, 1984).

The above discussion reflects the range of organisational contexts within which struggles for racial equality and racial justice have been pursued: multiracial, anti-racist and civil rights organisations and groups; black organisations and groups and finally mainstream political parties. Organisations thus constitute the means by which individuals and groups have access to the state beyond channels which permit individual access. The nature of these links with the state depends on the organisation in question although all organisations can be characterised in terms of the extent of their exclusion from the formal status of the state.

The variety of strategies including spontaneous responses which are characteristic of these organisations, groups and constituencies, such as protests, marches, resolutions, petitioning, lobbying, representations and street conflicts, must be seen in part to be a dimension of the relationship between organisations and the contexts in which racial inequalities are structured through political intervention and practice. Strategies too are a function of ideologies: what is and isn't considered legitimate, effective and/or desirable in terms of action. The varying strategies referred to above are linked to particular perceptions of the race 'problem'. Although racial inequalities are commonly acknowledged, the source of these inequalities and relatedly the most effective means to tackle them, beg a series of questions around which there is no clear consensus. What is more, there is no easy way of ascribing ideological positions to particular organisations or groups or factions. Invariably these positions become defined and redefined in the course of struggle and debate, and differences which emerge are contingent on a number of factors, of which allegiance to some general ideological stance is but one.

Legislation and racial equality

The Race Relations Acts   The best known government attempts to combat racial discrimination are the three Race Relations Acts of 1965, 1968 and 1976. Each of the Acts, all passed under Labour governments, sought to eliminate discrimination both by recourse to the sanction of the courts and through persuasion and public education. In other words the Acts contained a combination of coercive powers and promotional strategies. The 1965 Act established the Race Relations Board to act on complaints of alleged discrimination in places of public resort. The then newly established National Committee for Commonwealth Immigrants (NCCI) on the other hand was more concerned with liaison, educational and coordinating activities. Local voluntary liaison committees, the forerunners of Community Relations Councils, emerged from the mid-sixties, and the Act sought to coordinate their work and utilise their local knowledge in the administration and implementation of the Act. The role of the pressure group CARD (the Campaign Against Racial Discrimination) was significant in both promoting the Bill and in influencing its detailed provisions.

The 1968 Race Relations Act extended the remit of the Act to include housing and employment. The very significant PEP study of that time had confirmed racial discrimination varying in extent 'from the massive to the substantial' (Daniel, 1968, p. 209). The Act replaced the NCCI with the Community Relations Commission and the membership and functions of the Race Relations Board and its regional conciliation committees were increased and extended.

The most recent Race Relations Act, of 1976, once again sought to extend and refine previous legislation. It did so firstly by redefining discrimination to include the area of indirect as well as direct discrimination. The former referred to cases where unjustifiable practices and procedures which apply to everyone have the effect of putting people of a particular racial group at a disadvantage (Race Relations Act, para. 1). Secondly it reformed the complaints procedure so that individuals henceforth had the right to take individual cases of complaint to an Industrial Tribunal or County Court without having to await the decision of the Race Relations

Board. The third most significant change in point of fact was the abolition of the Race Relations Board and the Community Relations Commission and their replacement by the Commission for Racial Equality which, like the Equal Opportunities Commission in the field of sex discrimination, performs both coercive and promotional functions.

Section 11 of the Local Government Act 1966   S11 is the most long-standing of central government policies available to support local race related initiatives. The provision entitles certain local authorities to claim grant aid from central government in respect of the employment of staff to meet the needs of ethnic minorities. To be precise Section 11 made financial support available to:

> Local authorities who . . . are required to make special provision in the exercise of any of their functions in consequence of the presence within their areas of substantial numbers of immigrants from the Commonwealth whose language or customs differ from those of the community, grants of such amounts as he may with the consent of the Treasury determine on account of expenditure of such descriptions (being expenditure in respect of the employment of staff), as he may so determine. (Section 11, Local Government Act, 1966.)

In 1979 the Labour government sought to revise Section 11 through the introduction of the Local Government Grants (Ethnic Groups) Bill. The government fell before the Bill was passed. The Conservative government did not pursue Labour's plans for separate legislation. New guidelines, however, were introduced (Home Office, 1982; 1983) which attempted to overcome some of the anomalies and deficiencies in the grant system. The rule, whereby only local authorities with immigrant populations which had arrived within the previous 10 years could apply, was abolished. Given rigid immigration controls, this would have increasingly meant that most authorities, over time would not be in a position to claim. Other authorities, too, such as Cardiff and Liverpool who had long settled black populations became eligible for the first time to claim monies. All new post holders funded under Section 11 were asked to be identified individually, in the past the monies had been applied for in block form – without any indication of specific posts, job responsibilities, etc. Finally local authorities were asked to consult with local 'Commonwealth immigrant communities' before making their applications for grant aid.

Policies for the inner city   Like Section 11, policies for the inner city have sought to provide additional resources through grant aid to those areas of relatively high urban deprivation. The first Urban Programme therefore, of 1968, was designed to alleviate those areas of 'special need'. No attempt was made to clarify 'special needs' or to identify the criteria for selecting particular areas and projects for funding. Nevertheless it was clear from the outset that race had in some way been a factor in the thinking behind and the practical workings of the programmed. In terms of its origins the introduction of the Urban Programme has been linked to racial conflict or the threat of racial conflict. Examples from both the United States and Britain were cited in political debate in the late 1960s, the best known of which were the fears of racial bloodbaths expressed most forcefully at that time by Enoch Powell. Despite these connections, some of which were loosely drawn in Harold Wilson's May Day address in 1968 when the Urban Programme was introduced for the first time, the relationship between urban deprivation and racial disadvantage was never established and so precise policy implications have remained consistently ambiguous.

The initiative which was intended to supersede the Urban Programme, outlined in the Inner City White Paper (DoE, 1977b) was no less ambiguous on the issue of racial disadvantage than its predecessor. The main concern in the new inner city initiative was to shift the emphasis towards the so-called structural aspects of urban deprivation, that is to say economic decline and physical decay of the environment. Although once again the issue of race featured prominently in parliamentary debates on the White Paper, the latter could not itself decide how far racial minorities should be regarded as a specific dimension of urban disadvantage or how far racial disadvantage was coterminous with urban deprivation which affected all inner city dwellers. In practice resources have been allocated to two types of areas. Those suffering most acute forms of deprivation such as Liverpool, receive funding through one of the Inner City Partnerships, other authorities, such as Wolverhampton, receive monies through the submission of a rolling inner area programme. In line with the intended shift in emphasis, local authorities are required to give priority to applications proposing economic and environmental schemes. Central government pays 75 per cent of the expensive costs incurred by local authorities in funding its assortment of local schemes and projects.

Broadening the analysis of anti-racist politics

What has been attempted so far in this section is a review of what are generally regarded in current literature to be the principal forms of political opposition and legislative response to racial inequality. We would argue that both are restrictive in terms of their conception of politics and policy and the relationship between the two. Debates surrounding political opposition are thus confined to racism's most explicit manifestations for example in immigration policy, policing and extreme right wing organisations. Legislation (as a form of central policy) on the other hand, is generally discussed in terms of a number of relatively high profile central government race related initiatives. More significantly perhaps, in the case of the latter, is the interpretation invariably lent to these initiatives. In our review above we have merely described some of their more salient legal and administrative characteristics. We did not assume, as does much of the literature, that all such initiatives must be viewed with suspicion at the very least or more reasonably as devices designed to defuse racial conflict and black protest thereby to control and weaken any form of militant response from below. Not only then is the analysis restricted in terms of the range of policies it addresses. It makes no attempt to differentiate between 'positive' and 'negative' forms and effects of policies. All are treated as part of a homogeneous bloc, the product of a monolithic state machine.

There are a number of reasons for broadening the above conception of politics and policy and breaking with the mechanistic view of policy and the state common to much of the literature. First such a broader conception creates the possibility for developing an analysis of and strategies for combating racism in perhaps less obvious or explicit political contexts than those of immigration but which are no less significant in terms of their effects. Policies (or the lack of them) on employment, housing, families, taxation, health and social security and education all have their own modes of operation which once identified could be challenged in various ways through political action.

Secondly the broader conception of policy and the abandonment of the monolithic principle means that mainstream policies can now be conceived in terms of the development of positive programmes contributing to racial equality. Racial equality is thus not just about marginal initiatives made available to black groups through grant aid and through inner city policy. It is about changing the structure of provision of, say, mainstream housing policy, to ensure that racial minorities are not excluded from certain types of tenure, that properties are available which are appropriate to different cultural groupings or that racial minorities are represented at least in proportionate numbers in the workings of all levels of the housing system.

Thirdly it permits a breakdown of the political and policy making processes in terms of local, regional and national levels of state activity; between different policies which have their own relatively distinct modes of operation, and between different political forces (power blocs, alliances, etc.) both inside and outside the formal apparatus of the local state. What we are suggesting in the chapters which follow is that the above do not necessarily perform or operate in a unitary and undifferentiated way. This allows for a more complex analysis of the politics, including policy development. The 1976 Race Relations Act for instance can be seen not so much as a diversionary and divisive instrument, but rather as a legal weapon, blunt but sharper than its predecessors, and borne of pressure from local organisations in their submissions to select committees, research evidence produced by PEP (Smith, 1977) and a desire (voiced by the civil service in particular) to bring race relations legislation into line with the law on sex discrimination. The Act thus provides the opportunity for a more effective analysis of current and future strategic intervention in policy making and the role of campaigns, organisations, research and other political forces in that process. Finally in breaking down the state and the policy making/implementation process in this way, it creates the possibility of variations in local use and implementation of 'positive' and 'negative' central policies. Section 11 has proved a good illustration of these vertical and horizontal forms of unevenness.

Finally the differentiation of policy brings a number of current issues within the legitimate boundaries of social scientific discussion and analysis. What are equal opportunity policies? How can they operate, how far do they work? What is monitoring? Why is the keeping of ethnic records significant? How can they be used positively? What role does race relations machinery in local town halls play in combatting racial inequality? Could it be more effective? These are questions which are invariably eschewed or reforms which are invariably dismissed in current literature on the politics of race. Race related reforms, whether these take the form of policy statements, administrative procedures, committee structures or town hall appointments, can constitute conditions for racial equality. The efficacy of these reforms and the outcomes of the struggles which emerge around them are contingent and neither is amenable to prediction or dismissable in any priori way.

Conclusions

We have attempted in this chapter to provide the basis for a political analysis of race which escapes the narrow confines of both politics on the one hand and policy issues on the other. An acknowledgement of the deficiencies of both taken on their own, can lead us towards a more complex analysis of the integral role of policy in the institutionalisation of racism and the need to identify specific political including policy mechanisms responsible for the creation and perpetuation of racial inequalities. We shall develop these connections in the next chapter as well as providing a review of existing evidence of inequalities, since we take this to be the starting point of our own political involvement in the issue of race.

3 Institutionalised Racism and Public Policy

Institutional racism, in our view, is the measure of systematic inequality which results from institutional processes which are racially discriminatory. The control of black immigration (through legislation) and the evidence of racial harassment and violence are the sharp end of institutional racism, and because of this they have consistently been the focus of anti-racist activity. While cases of harassment and victimisation abound (and these are documented throughout the anti-racist and black press) there exist a variety of other, sometimes more subtle, forms of institutionalised discrimination. What we shall be arguing and building a case for in this chapter is a more detailed exploration of institutionalised racism. In doing so we shall begin to evolve a framework which could be applicable to a variety of institutional contexts: a framework which begins with the reality of racial inequalities, in terms of differences of condition between black and white, and traces these back through the institutional context in which they ultimately find expression. The focus of our discussion will be on the politics and policies of these institutional contexts since these provide the sites for anti-racist struggles and hence potentially of positive change. This more detailed framework will allow us to identify specific forms of local institutionalised racism, that is to say, inequalities which result from processes initiated locally and over which local governments, bureaucracies, and firms for example have some measure of control.

The framework for analysing the details of institutionalised racism consists of a series of analytical principles. These include locating: the specific institutional means by which inequalities are generated or reinforced; the settings in which these inequalities are realised (both in terms of decision-making and implementation); and the kinds of internal procedures which legitimate and permit these forms of institutionalised discrimination. These internal structures can in turn be related to external conditions, such as to legal or policy frameworks as well as racial ideologies which serve to support and legitimate institutional practice.

Within institutional settings themselves we shall distinguish policies which provide a framework of rules, principles and regulations, from administrative practices which refer to the interpretation and application of policy. The interconnection of these and their articulation with the kinds of external conditions referred to above provide the basis for our analysis of racism or strictly speaking, racisms, which are institutionally specific and which sometimes fall under local control. Any effective challenge to these inequalities must in our view take account of the institutional forms and processes which underpin them. It has been too easy in the past for those reluctant to acknowledge racism within their own institutional ranks and blind to reality of racial inequalities which result, to ignore or deflect those who challenge their professional judgement and/or moral stance.

The chapter is organised into two main sections. The first is devoted to a review of survey and research evidence identifying the nature and extent of racial inequalities and their links with public provision and policy. In the second part of the chapter, which focuses more closely on local policy and its role in the production and maintenance of racial inequalities, we use examples from our own research practice to illustrate four 'forms' of policy which effectively institutionalise racism. The conclusions set the scene for a closer look (in Chapter 3) at local politics as an arena of struggle.

Racial inequalities: an overview of recent evidence

When we use the terms 'black' or 'racial' in this book we are not seeking to provide definitions which are universal or exclusive. On the contrary we have restricted our usage to Great Britain, the post-World War II period and to Afro-Caribbean and Asian immigrants and their descendants. The acknowledged differences and variations between and within these groups should not detract from evidence which points to systematic inequalities of condition and treatment and between black and white people living in post-war Britain. It is these inequalities and the political processes surrounding them, including that of struggle, which have conferred a political status on black people which we have taken as the starting point of our analysis.

Conditions of racial inequality – the private sector

According to figures published in the official *Employment Gazette* (DoE, June 1984) the unemployment rate was 20.6 per cent for West Indian men, 16.9 per cent for Asian men and 9.7 per cent for white men. The figures for the respective groups of women were 14.5 per cent, 17.9 per cent and 8.7 per cent.

The government study attributed these differences, in the main, to discrimination, since only a small part could be linked to age distribution and level of educational qualifications (*Runnymede Trust Bulletin*, September 1984).

Press Wine Bar, Wolverhampton

A Wolverhampton Industrial Tribunal found that a 24-year-old Jamaican, Miss Jennifer Cooper, had been unlawfully discriminated against by the Press Wine Bar in Wolverhampton. The Wine Bar was then owned by Mr P R Fort who was the respondent in this case.

The tribunal found that Miss Cooper, who had a City & Guilds Catering Certificate, tried on three separate occasions to obtain a job as a part-time kitchen worker. Each time she was untruthfully told that the job had been filled.

The tribunal said Mr Fort repeatedly lied to Miss Cooper about the job. Although Miss Cooper's representative had asked for only £150 in compensation, the industrial tribunal awarded Miss Cooper £200 for injury to feeling.

The case had been referred to the Commission by Wolverhampton Community Relations Council.

(*CRE*, 1984c, p. 43)

The extent of unemployment amongst the young age cohorts of Afro-Caribbean and Asian descent is even higher, and more disproportionate, than in the case of all age groups. There is evidence here too that discrimination is a major contributory factor. When black people do find work they find it predominantly in low paid blue collar occupations characterised by a relatively poor physical working environment, including great risks to health and safety, working unsocial hours, with fewer prospects of promotion

In a period of high unemployment among young people in the country as a whole, young black people are particularly vulnerable and suffer disproportionately high levels of unemployment. In 1982 the Government's 'Social Trends' indicated that, while 25 per cent of young people aged 16–19 were unemployed, the figure for ethnic minorities was 50 per cent. The Commission regards this differentially high level of unemployment as profoundly damaging and accords high priority to work in this area.

(*CRE*, 1984c, p. 73)

Discrimination cases

Two black teenage girls received more than £1,000 damages between them after they were discriminated against while on the government's Youth Training Scheme. Susan Warner and Denise Edmondson had been refused work at a hairdressing salon while six white colleagues were taken on. The case was taken to Birmingham industrial tribunal but was settled out of court.

Each girl received £300 compensation and £150 for loss of training opportunities. Warner received a further £25 for loss of earnings, and Edmondson a further £154. Wolverhampton Chamber of Commerce, the managing agents of the scheme, also paid £200 to each girl although denying discrimination (*Daily Telegraph* 4.4.84).

The case is the first to have been brought since the Youth Training Scheme was brought under the protection of the Race Relations Act (see *Bulletin* No. 160). The Commission for Racial Equality has since said that discrimination on YTS is 'widespread'. Statistics supplied by the Manpower Services Commission and evidence from employers, trade unions and others, show that a smaller proportion of black people obtain places on the better, Mode A, schemes where there is a greater chance of a permanent job. More are on Mode B schemes with fewer long term prospects. In London and the south-east, 45% of Afro-caribbeans are on Mode A schemes, compared with 70% of whites. In Merseyside, the figures are 24% and 49% (*Guardian* 6.4.84).

(*Race and Immigration:*
The Runnymede Trust Bulletin,
June 1984, pp. 3–4)

(which is one aspect of income increases) but greater chance of layoffs and redundancy (Brown, 1984, pp. 296–9).

Outside employment, and in the community, black people are subject to a variety of forms of unequal treatment. Disproportionate numbers of black people are the victims of assault and harassment and their property susceptible to criminal damage. *Racial Attacks*, a report carried out by the Home Office over a three month period in 1981, found rates of victimisation of 1.4 per hundred thousand of the population for whites, 51.2 for West Indians and Africans and 69.7 for Asians (Home Office, 1981). The PSI survey concluded that the Home Office figures if anything underestimated the differences which could be more than ten times the official figures (Brown, 1984). This is attributed to both the under-reporting of racial attacks, and the method of police classification which until the mid-1980s was determined at the discretion of the police (*Guardian*, 19.1.85).

As consumers in shops, restaurants, clubs, public houses and private agencies, it is not uncommon for black people in Britain to experience discrimination and abuse; and in a significant number of cases they are denied access altogether.

A comparison of 1971 and 1981 census data reveals continuing inequalities in the private housing market both in terms of levels of owner occupation, and in housing density and conditions. There is evidence too, that this restriction is at least in part the result of overt racial discrimination.

As consumers of the media, black people find themselves under-represented in terms of reporters, actors, producers, and writers, but over-represented in terms of a variety of stereotypical images in which they are projected: as young criminals, as illegal immigrants, as costly and burdensome, as perpetrators of social problems, as demanders of preferential treatment, as single parents, drug abusers and rioters. ~health~ ~inequality~

Conditions of racial inequality – the public sector

So far we have restricted our consideration of racial inequalities to the private sector. It might be hoped and expected that areas of institutional activity under exclusive public control might seek to ameliorate inequalities experienced outside. This, however, is not the case.

As employees, black people are under-represented at almost

Racial violence

Children have been among the victims of several serious racist attacks in recent weeks. On the last day of the school term in Tower Hamlets, east London, 14 year old Mukith Miah was attacked by a gang of 14 white youths as he walked to school. Mukith was punched, kicked unconscious and stabbed twice. One wound was 2 inches long, the other, down the centre of his back, 10 inches long. Mukith was rushed to a nearby hospital and was detained for several days. According to press reports, one white 13 year old has been charged with causing grievous bodily harm and two 15 year olds with causing actual bodily harm (*Asian Times* 3.8.84). (Mukith's mother, Sara Bibi, was herself the victim of racial attack two years ago.)

On 13 August, again in London's east end, a gang of 11 year olds attacked a 9 year old Asian boy, slashing him with a kitchen knife. The boy, who had been playing with friends in Limehouse, was surrounded by five boys on BMX bikes. According to one report, police said that he was lucky not to have lost his arm (*Sun* 13.8.84).

In Forest Gate, east London, a baby girl was shot through the temple by a sniper. Louisa Williams was being pushed in a pram by her mother when a passing car slowed down and a gun was fired. A pellet was removed from the baby's skull in an operation lasting three hours (*Newham Recorder* 19.7.84).

In north London, a 9 year old boy, who is half Asian, was attacked on his way home by a skinhead gang near an adventure playground in Islington. They ripped his clothes off and threw him into a bush (*Islington Gazette* 15.6.84).

Also in north London, an Asian youth club was invaded by a gang wielding knives, chains and iron bars. The incident occurred at the United Indian Youth Centre in Wembley. Most of the youths present managed to escape but two boys were assaulted. The gang also threw a fire extinguisher through the windscreen of a youth's car and damaged the bodywork (*New Life* 24.8.84).

In Bradford, two white youths were fined and bound over to keep the peace for a year for an unprovoked attack on an Asian youth. Richard Lumb admitted assaulting Javed Rashid while Stephen Waterhouse admitted using words or behaviour likely to cause a breach of the peace. The prosecution said that Lumb had seen Rashid in a doorway vomiting and had kicked him several times. Waterhouse had shouted encouragement. Rashid was detained overnight in hospital with cuts and bruises (*New Life* 3.8.84).

Harassment on housing estates

Meanwhile the harassment of black families on council estates in London has continued. In August, *Asian Times* highlighted the plight of the Mottlib family on the Hadrian House estate in Tower Hamlets, east London. The estate is scheduled for demolition but is presently occupied by five Asian families who fear moving to other estates which have records of racial violence. The Mottlibs have had their washing set on fire, gun pellets have been fired through their windows, and racial abuse is a regular occurrence. In one incident, a brick was thrown through a window, narrowly missing a two year old child (24.8.84).

Families from the Lincoln Estate, also in Tower Hamlets, have also been the victims of serious violence and harassment (see *Bulletin* No. 170), and in August tenants from the estate picketed the local council offices demanding action.

A recent report on the estate by the Greater London Council's Race and Housing Action Team described one meeting in May which was attended by 10 Bengali tenants and others. Nearly all the tenants, the report said, had experienced some form of attack either on themselves, their children or their property – 'stone, bricks, sand being thrown at adults and children; spitting, jostling, name calling; lighted fireworks, cigarettes, lighted matches, paper and other offensive material being put through the letter-box. All have experienced continual door-banging at all hours of the day and night. There have been eggs, dog excrement and other things daubed on the door and thrown at windows'.

The report also described a later meeting in July which had been attended by five police officers, including two senior officers. A white woman tenant declared that if the Bangladeshis could be collected together, she would petrol bomb them. None of the police, the report says, reacted to this. When questioned afterwards, a senior officer laughed the matter off and said that the woman had not dropped the bomb after all. Action would be taken after she had done so.

The report comments that this was an occasion when a few words from the police might have helped to discourage the woman from making racist remarks in the future. As it was, she and the more junior officers present must have gone away with the impression that such sentiments were perfectly acceptable to the higher ranks in the police.

The Race and Housing Action Team has made a number of recommendations about the handling of racial harassment. It proposes that the GLC pressure the police to investigate complaints promptly and sympathetically and take action to warn tenants of the possible consequences of racial harassment.

In Islington, north London, a report by the housing department to the Council's Race Relations Committee stated that in a three month period more than 30 cases of racial harassment had been reported to the council. Ten tenants were reported to have been transferred following complaints (*Islington Gazette* 6.7.84).

(*Race and Immigration: The Runnymede Trust Bulletin*, No. 172, October 1984)

Josephine's Nightclub, Sheffield

Messrs G Pearce, G Saunders, D Smith and Ms S Dacres all live in the Sheffield area, and are black.

During the Spring and Summer of 1982 the four were refused admission at various times by Josephine's Nightclub in Sheffield owned by A & S Entertainments Ltd.

Mr G Pearce and Ms Dacres were refused entry on 26 March 1982 when the doorman told them: "We've had problems with black people recently and we can't let you in". On 14 May 1982 Mr Saunders visited the premises with four white friends. His friends were allowed to enter but Mr Saunders was refused. He asked for an explanation and the doorman told him: "It's obvious isn't it?"

Mr D Smith, a former Sheffield Community Relations Officer, visited the Nightclub on 10 June 1982 with a white friend. Again the white friend was allowed into the Club, but Mr Smith was refused without explanation.

All four complainants were assisted by the Commission to bring legal proceedings before the Leeds County Court. Subsequently, A & S Entertainments decided not to defend themselves at a hearing and agreed a settlement which was submitted to judgment on 27 May 1983. The terms were as follows:

1. An admission that the Club unlawfully discriminated against Mr Pearce, Mr Saunders and Ms Dacres.
2. An apology to Mr D Smith for the treatment he received but no admission of unlawful discrimination.
3. An undertaking that the Club would not refuse entry to them or any other persons on grounds of race in the future.
4. Damages of £100 were paid to Mr Pearce, Mr Saunders and Ms Dacres, and a £50 ex gratia payment to Mr Smith
5. A & S Entertainments paid the Commission's legal costs.

(*CRE*, 1984c, p. 44)

---

every level and in every sector of public employment. In Westminster, and in many town halls up and down the country, in government as well as local authority departments, they are significant by their absence. In Liverpool for instance there are 272 black employees out of 29,918 despite their 7 per cent representation in the City as a whole. In Wolverhampton, in some departments, there is no representation at all. For example, and despite the significance of unemployment amongst young black people, there are no black careers officers.

Black people are not only unequally treated as producers of public services, local authority employees, but also as consumers. They are disproportionately represented amongst the homeless and amongst those experiencing delays on council waiting lists. They are similarly over represented amongst those living in below

Housing statistics

Black families are still far more likely to be living in overcrowded conditions than white households, according to the 1981 Census. This shows that over 19% of families with a head of household born in the New Commonwealth or Pakistan live at a density of more than one person per room, compared with only 2% of UK families (excluding those born in the Irish republic). (The figures for New Commonwealth households do not include those headed by a black person who was born in this country.)

Far fewer black families live in privately rented accommodation than in 1971. Sixty one per cent of New Commonwealth householders are now owner occupiers and 24% are council tenants. Of the latter, 44% are Caribbeans compared with only 26% in 1971. The percentage of Asian council tenants has risen from 4% in 1971 to 13% in 1981, still much lower than the 29% of council tenants in the population as a whole.

The high proportion of owner occupiers amongst Asian households can be deceptive as far as living standards are concerned. Whilst 76% of Asian families own their own home, overcrowding (that is more than one person per room), runs at 38% and 40% in Pakistani and Bangladeshi-headed households respectively. This compares with just over 1% for families with a head of household born in the UK. In addition, over 10% of Pakistani or Bangladeshi owner-occupiers lack an inside WC or bath compared with 3% of UK-born home owners. (*Housing and Household Tables*, Census 1981, HMSO)

(*Race and Immigration: The Runnymede Trust Bulletin*, December 1983, p. 4)

average accommodation in terms of basic amenities as well as being victims of harassment and abuse on council estates.

As pupils and students in our educational system, children of Afro-Caribbean descent in particular figure disproportionately in

Mr and Mrs Carnell

Ms Theresa Jones is black, 19-years-old and Sheffield born. During May 1982 she attempted to find private rented accommodation for herself in Sheffield.

During May, Ms Jones saw a series of newspaper advertisements offering accommodation suitable for single females. Ms Jones realised subsequently that the flats and bedsits were all owned by Mr and Mrs Carnell of Ryegate Road, Sheffield 10. Ms Jones made two visits to Ryegate Road, on 21 May and 25 May, to enquire about accommodation. On the first occasion she was told by Mrs Carnell that the flat had been rented already, and on the second that the flat was amongst elderly residents and they were looking for an older person. As she left Ryegate Road on 25 May, Ms Jones recalled seeing a white acquaintance walking towards the Carnell's house. A few weeks later Mr Jones found out that the white woman was given the flat and that she was only 18-years-old.

The Commission supported Ms Jones in taking legal proceedings before the Leeds County Court and spent many months making enquiries in an attempt to locate the white acquaintance. After the Commission had secured this evidence, Mr and Mrs Carnell decided not to defend their case at a hearing. They agreed a settlement which was submitted to judgment on the following terms:

1. An admission of unlawful discrimination;
2. An undertaking not to repeat such action in the future;
3. A payment to Ms Jones of the sum of £175 damages for injury to her feelings.

(*CRE*, 1984c, p. 46)

Housing advice staff employed by Northampton council racially discriminated for several years, according to a council document leaked in October. The system involved marking cards with white dots to indicate to staff not to send black people to private landlords who had said that they would not accept black tenants. The practice was stopped only after a housing advice worker complained to the council's chief executive last October (*Guardian* 27.10.84).

(*Race and Immigration: The Runnymede Trust Bulletin*, December 1984)

---

lower streams of our inner city comprehensive schools (Townsend and Brittan, 1972); in special units for disruptive children (Tomlinson, 1983, pp. 42 ff) and in the MSC's Youth Training Scheme's

The Report by Community Relations Commission *Reporting Race* deals with the role and responsibility of the press in reporting race relations during 1976, and explicitly says: 'The vast majority of the British reading public gain their newspaper information from the *Daily Mirror*, *The Sun*, *Daily Express*, *Daily Mail* and *Daily Telegraph* in that order. Apart from notable exceptions in the *Daily Mirror* those newspapers were most likely to sensationalise some or all of the issues during the period covered ... Although the *Daily Telegraph*, *Daily Express*, *Daily Mail*, *Daily Mirror*, and *The Sun* were responsible for the most sensational headlines during this period *The Times*, *Guardian* and *Financial Times* did not resist the temptation either. For two weeks readers were subjected to an almost constant news coverage on Asian immigration from all the newspapers – and these two weeks turned out to be only the precursor of a long summer in which immigration, race relations and black people provided a major portion of news coverage ... A clear example of sensational reporting of race relations has been the way in which the majority of the press has treated Enoch Powell's speeches over the past years. The reasons for this are clear: one overriding principle for newspaper editors is to keep circulation figures high and this is usually met by printing what will keep the readers interested. Mr Powell's speeches are sensational. The majority of papers, particularly the popular press, have therefore correlated readers' interest with Mr Powell's speeches and have placed them accordingly: with front page headlines. In addition to giving these speeches priority, and in some cases as a consequence of this priority, the general impression given by many newspapers has been one of tacit approval of his views. The argument is to some extent a circular one – do readers give a high priority to Mr Powell's speeches because the newspapers do? It is also a question of responsible reporting on the hyper-sensitive issue of race relations. If editors and journalists are to carry out their responsibilities in interpretative and balanced reporting of this issue, speeches from Enoch Powell should be considered carefully in terms of their position and treatment in the newspaper and should be accompanied by accounts of the alternative points of view'.

(*Race and the Media*, CRE, 1983a, p. 16)

Mode B (CRE, 1984d). They are under-represented on degree courses and in universities (*Education for All*, 1985, ch. 3).

Against the background of conditions reviewed above, certain public services are particularly significant for black people. Both health and social services fall into this category. However, problems surrounding proof of identity and entitlement to use of the services have inhibited rather than facilitated institutional access.

The rights of social security claimants are constantly threatened by a set of rules governing the administration of social security and the interpretation of those rules both of which effectively discrimi-

Council housing discrimination

Black council tenants in Hackney live in worse conditions than whites because of direct discrimination, according to the results of a formal investigation by the Commission for Racial Equality. Although black and white council residents have equal access to council housing in Hackney, black tenants live in accommodation which is inferior by all measures used by the investigators.

This inequality could not be accounted for by the procedures and practices of the council, nor by any social difference between the black and white tenants. The Commission therefore concluded that direct racial discrimination was the main reason why black applicants were being given lower quality housing.

Background

The CRE began its four year investigation into Hackney's housing policies in 1978 as part of its overall strategy on housing. Hackney was singled out for the Commission's first investigation into public housing because of its large ethnic minority population (19% of the borough are black) and not because of any alleged acts of discrimination by the council. As one of the most economically deprived boroughs in Britain, with a decreasing supply of available council housing, the demands on Hackney Council stock are considerable.

Findings

The investigation looked at a sample of 1,292 Hackney council tenants from the main channels of access into council housing over a two year period. Two run-down estates were also examined in detail, as well as the role of the Greater London Council in rehousing Hackney's homeless people. The investigation of each of these areas involved interviews with housing staff and all tenants, a review of the council's policies and practices, and an examination of the housing files.

Black tenants on the waiting list were especially discriminated against. While the proportion of black and white tenants on the waiting list sample was very similar (45% black; 49% white), black families were three times less likely to be offered a house, rather than a flat or maisonette, than white families in similar circumstances.

White families were over eight times more likely to be offered a new property than black families (25% compared to 3%), while black families were three times more likely to be offered pre-war property (24% compared to 7.5%).

Of all the new property given to waiting list tenants 88% went to whites and only 12% to blacks. A third indicator used to measure the quality of accommodation was that of floor levels. Over a third of white applicants received low floor levels, compared to less than one fifth of black applicants.

The investigation also found evidence of discrimination in the housing of the homeless, those applying for a transfer, and tenants whose property was under compulsory purchase, although this discrimination was less marked than for waiting list tenants.

The in-depth study of two run-down estates in Hackney showed that in both cases black tenants were moving in as white ones moved out. The study of the homeless quota housed by the GLC revealed that it was Turks and Greeks who were disproportionately living in older properties, although this could have been accounted for by family size. In all other cases the differences could not be accounted for by family size, age, rent arrears, medical requirements, applicants' preferences or familiarity with the system. The report concluded that discrimination must have taken place by the allocating officers who were able correctly to differentiate the ethnic origin of the applicants in 60% of cases (38% through specific references on the files) even though no formal ethnic monitoring system had been instituted at the time.

Remedies

Hackney council co-operated with the investigation throughout and since a non-discrimination notice was issued in May 1983, have introduced changes in training and recruitment, altered the disciplinary code, and created a sub-committee of the Housing Committee to oversee the council's compliance with the non-discrimination notice. Ethnic monitoring was introduced by the council in December 1982.

The CRE will be visiting over 40 local authorities during 1984 to discuss the implications of the report.

(*Race and Council Housing in Hackney: report of a formal investigation*, CRE, 1984)

(*Race and Immigration: The Runnymede Trust Bulletin*, September 1984)

nate against circumstances more commonly experienced by black people. Not only is access to the service provision frustrated because of doubts over eligibility, etc., but invariably the nature of provision itself effectively works to exclude black people.

Elsewhere in the field of health and social services inequalities are maintained. There is a relative absence of elderly black people in residential establishments and an absence of health provision which responds directly to the needs of racial minorities. In other services the existence of a disproportionate number of racial minorities itself is a reflection of inequalities experienced elsewhere for example in the greater numbers of young black children in residential care and likewise in the numbers of black youth attending statutory and voluntary aided youth clubs.

The system of legal and judicial administration, which might be expected to be working to protect, secure and guarantee the rights of black people is ironically adding one further dimension to those inequalities referred to above.

Disproportionate numbers of young black people are stopped by the police on suspicion of committing a criminal offence. Of these a disproportionate number are subsequently arrested and subsequently released on grounds of insufficient evidence.

In addition to evidence of injustices within the judicial and legal

Discrimination in housing

An award-winning investigation into the allocation of council housing in Birmingham has again highlighted discrimination in the public sector against black people.

The research, carried out by Jeff Henderson and Valerie Karn who were awarded the Donald Robertson Memorial Prize 1983, reached the following conclusions with regard to ethnic minorities:

– despite previous evidence that a five year residential qualification had been the greatest barrier to the eligibility of ethnic minorities for public housing, the reduction to two years residence has not made it any less difficult for blacks to qualify.

– blacks who do receive housing are given older housing than whites. For example, 5% of white two member households were given pre-1919 housing compared to 28% of Asian two member households. Similarly 5% of white four member households compared to 42% of Asian four member households were given pre-1919 housing.

– Afro-Caribbeans with children are more likely to receive a flat instead of a house than are whites with the same number of children.

– whites obtain a disproportionate number of transfers and therefore gain access to more and newer housing.

– Afro-Caribbeans have their area preference met less often than whites. Asians' preferences are met more frequently than Afro-Caribbeans', but this may be because their recorded area preferences are limited to a very few districts which already have large numbers of resident Asians.

– following from this, despite the housing department's stated intention to encourage blacks to move into 'white estates', those blacks who did express a preference to do so, were less likely to have their preferences met than white applicants for the same estate, or black applicants for 'black estates'.

– blacks were found to be less satisfied with properties allocated to them than whites, and this dissatisfaction related to the condition of the property.

How discrimination occurs

The intention of the survey was not merely to produce more evidence of discrimination against black people in the allocation of public housing, as this has already been well documented, but to try to discover exactly how and why discrimination occurs.

Apart from the period between 1969 and 1975 when Birmingham tried to disperse ethnic minority applicants into all types of housing and geographical areas, the city has had no specific policy with regard to the housing of ethnic minorities. The survey, therefore, turned from a study of formal policies to look at the informal decision-making processes on the part of housing employees, which was where, it was thought, discrimination must have been occurring.

The authors were not concerned with 'racial discrimination in isolation . . . but rather with the specification of the ways in which discriminatory ideologies and practices based on race, class and gender combined in particular . . . circumstances.' They argued that it was necessary to look at the behaviour of housing department personnel in the context of their existence within an inegalitarian society which perpetuates ideological myths and stereotypes. Race (as well as class and gender) discrimination is inevitable when personnel are seen as influenced by the wider society's attitudes as to who is and is not 'respectable', and therefore who is or is not 'deserving' of favourable treatment with regard to the allocation of scarce housing resources.

The so-called 'points system' only provides a very generalised picture of who is in the greatest need. Many people will have the same amount of 'points' and deciding on allocations at this level is where stereotyped assumptions leading to discrimination will do the damage.

Housing personnel who hold to stereotyped ideas (consciously or unconsciously), may find it necessary to do so in order to rationalize for themselves the difficult decisions they make on a day to day basis which have a great effect on other peoples lives.

The report found considerable evidence that 'stereotyped' views held by housing department personnel of working class and single parent applicants resulted in discriminatory treatment, but that black working class and black single parent families received even worse treatment. For example, only 22% of white one parent families were allocated houses rather than flats, while 44% of two parent white families were. However the figures for Afro-Caribbeans were only 17% (one parent) and 38% (two parent). The combination of race and a particular family status (which was perceived as not 'respectable') compounded the discriminatory treatment.

Conclusion

The authors conclude that the prospects for ending discrimination in the allocation of public housing are not good. This is firstly because of the importance they place on seeing the judgements of housing department employees as based on their views of 'respectability' (where 'race' is intermingled with attitudes towards class, family status etc). Therefore tackling racial discrimination on its own is not realistic. Secondly, from a practical point of view, even adopting a positive policy of giving those who aren't 'respectable' the best housing would only lead to 'respectable' people opting out of the public housing sector altogether, thus stigmatizing public housing and those who use it even further.

(J. Henderson and V. Karn: 'Race, Class and the Allocation of Public Housing in Britain', *Urban Studies* 21, 1984.)

(*Race and Immigration: The Runnymede Trust Bulletin*, September 1984, pp. 1–2)

---

systems, numerous studies have reported complaints of police harassment, brutality, and in the case of victims of assault, of police indifference and inaction.

The safety net which might be expected to be provided by such last resort agencies as social security and the police, is invariably absent. The role of these agencies is often not so much a defender but more a usurper of those rights. Rather than working to reduce the effects of various forms of inequality resulting from public and private spheres these agencies work to reinforce them.

Racial inequalities and local policy

A critical task for the development of effective anti-racist strategies is the reconstruction of those processes which can be

Race and social security

Racism and sexism pose additional barriers to Asians trying to claim welfare benefits, a recent report of a benefits 'takeup' campaign has concluded. The report of the Sandwell Benefits Take-Up Campaign (funded by the West Midlands County Council and Sandwell Metropolitan Borough Council) identified a number of problems which people of Asian origin face in claiming benefits.

The report says that the 1980 Social Security Act has effectively discriminated against black people and particularly against black immigrants. Evidence suggests, the report says, that the Department of Health and Social Security no longer applies the criteria for benefit evenly to all sections of society but 'has been granted powers to interfere into the lives of the Asian minorities who do make a claim (for example passport checks), or by asking them very personal questions which are not asked of the indigenous population'. The result of the linking of immigration status to entitlement to benefit has meant that many black claimants face 'particularly vigorous scrutiny'.

Passport checking, which is required in certain cases under the social security regulations, not only causes a 'great deal of difficulty and anxiety' but deters people who have a right to claim from doing so. In addition, the report says, passport checking is paradoxical. On the one hand passports are checked frequently, yet the DHSS will not accept them as verification of dates of birth. Instead, methods of proof are required, for example 'family record books' or 'birthday books', which many Asian people will simply not possess.

The report also deals with the 'quality of service' provided to the Asian community. While it acknowledges that the DHSS did translate the 'Cash Help' leaflet into various Asian languages some years ago, the report says that this did not prove very beneficial due to the lack of publicity and lack of distribution. The present plans to translate the 'Which Benefit' leaflet is welcomed, but the report points out that there are many other leaflets which also ought to be translated.

The report also criticises the use of the postal B1 claim form. This has 74 questions and requires a certain degree of English if it is to be completed correctly. Errors in completing it mean that a claim is delayed with the result that the claimant is expected to live on a reduced income until it is sorted out.

Assumptions made by DHSS officials about the Asian community are also criticised. These include the assumption that because the Asian community is seen as being close knit, people will easily be able to borrow money, either from relatives or friends or from temples. The report points out that temples do not lend money, and that high unemployment among black peoples makes it difficult for people to lend money even if they wish to.

The take up campaign found that many Asian women had little knowledge or understanding of welfare benefits. In addition they faced problems caused by the social security system itself. Some of these have been remedied by the recent implementation of the equal treatment provisions which allow either partner to claim for the couple, but other problems persist. For example, the report states, many Asian women who wish to separate from, or divorce, their husbands, will remain living in the same house to minimise the stigma attached to the breakup of the marriage. As a result they are then required to submit to lengthy interviews of a highly personal nature about their relationship with their husband. In addition, the report says, Asian women are expected to produce extra documentation when claiming and are required to show that they cannot obtain support from relatives or the community.

The report makes a number of recommendations including an end to passport checking, the translation of several leaflets, a 'massive media campaign' to advise people of their rights, and the appointment by local authorities of specialist welfare rights advisers.

English speakers only?

Extensive translation of social security material is also recommended in a recent report on claimants whose first language is not English. The report, by Maryrose Tarpey for Islington Peoples Rights, found that many Bengalis and Greek Cypriots interviewed were not familiar with the benefit system and that there was a general fear of claiming because of the 'trouble' this might cause. This was so even though everyone interviewed appeared to be in the country legally and to be fully entitled to claim. This problem was additional to the language difficulties which many had in claiming.

The report recommends also that the DHSS monitor take-up among ethnic minorities with the aim of maximising claims and ensuring that language and literacy do not prevent people from claiming, that the relationship between immigration status and entitlement to benefit be clarified and explained publicly to correct misconceptions which deter claims, and that local authorities appoint specialist welfare rights workers to work with minority communities.

Report of the Sandwell Welfare Rights Take-Up Campaign with Respect to Asian Minorities (from Welfare Rights Team, Economic Development Unit, County Hall, 1 Lancaster Circus, Queensway, Birmingham B4 7DJ)
English Speakers Only: a report of work on take-up of social security benefits with people whose first language is not English (Islington Peoples Rights, 324 St Paul's Road, London N1, send sae)

(*Race and Immigration: The Runnymede Trust Bulletin*, October 1984, pp. 2–3)

seen to underpin those inequalities reviewed above. In each case we need to establish the overall institutional context (in terms of an analysis of policies and their administration) which can be related directly or indirectly to racial inequality. In the case of *public* policy, we have argued that of all instruments of positive social change, *it* has a particular responsibility in terms of securing group rights and offering minorities protection from abuse and injustice. For those groups whose rights are constantly threatened in a variety of ways, positive institutional support is thus all the more crucial, particularly from local public institutions which are often most strategically placed to redress racial inequalities. In our experience however, not only is such support rarely forthcoming but in many ways local policies reinforce rather than challenge racial inequalities.

In this section we distinguish four ways in which local policy and administrative practice have effectively played this reinforcing role. At times as we shall see it is played more consciously and

Stop and search

A report published by the Home Office Research and Planning Unit earlier this year (Carole Willis: *The Use, Effectiveness and Impact of Police Stop and Search Powers*) showed that black men are two to three times more likely than white men to be stopped and searched by the police.

The study was based on research carried out in two areas of London (Kensington and Peckham), Watford and Luton. It found that the stop rate per 100 males in Kensington was 62, but for black males it was 149. In Peckham, the overall rate was 27, but for black men 60. In Watford the stop rate was 9, but 32 for black men. Even in Luton which had the lowest stop rate of 3, the stop rate for black men was still much higher at 10. In the two London areas, black men between the ages of 16 and 24 were stopped 10 times as often as the general average.

Of course, as the figures cited early show, relatively few of those stopped by the police are arrested or charged.

Willis found that it was not possible to calculate with any accuracy the number of stops which led to arrest but information on the number of prosecutions which resulted from stops was available. This showed that, with one exception, black men were again more likely to be prosecuted than their white counterparts. In Peckham, 8% of males stopped were prosecuted, but the figure for black males was 9% and for black men aged between 16 and 24, it was 10%. In Watford the figures were similar, 2, 3 and 4% respectively. The difference was most marked in Kensington where 8% of all males stopped were prosecuted, but 15% of all black men were prosecuted, rising to 18% in the case of black men aged between 16 and 24. Only in Luton were black men *less* likely to be prosecuted.

(*Race and Immigration: The Runnymede Trust Bulletin*, November 1983)

more directly than at others. How far policies are unwittingly embarked upon and implemented, how far they result in inequalities by design or default, and finally how far they result from the actions of one individual or represent a collective institutional response, are questions which will recur throughout this discussion. The answers to them confirm the integral relationship between public policy and inequality and the need to develop a framework both for the analysis of institutional racism and subsequently for an analysis of the politics of anti-racism.

Policies and practices which fail to redress racial injustice

In 1981 a black council tenant living in Wolverhampton wrote to the local housing department, complaining that rubbish had been tipped into his back garden, that windows had been broken and that his children had been taunted and physically assaulted on their way to school. Despite complaints to the police there had been little or no reduction in the nature and extent of victimisation. The housing department replied stating that there was little that could be done to support or protect his family from such attacks.

In 1982 a black stall keeper in Wolverhampton's market complained to the local market manager of constant abuse and harassment from fellow stall keepers and of one case of physical assault. As a result of an investigation into the particular incident he was banned from using market facilities for two days. He has subsequently taken further complaints to the market manager who has on occasions refused to meet with him. He has taken his complaints to the chairman of the Markets and Trading Committee of the local authority as yet to no effect.

In 1982 a black school teacher in Wolverhampton (one of the few black secondary school teachers in the town) received a final warning from the Director of Education for alleged negligence and incompetence. Complaints made by parents and children, some with racial imputations (the fact that she was an English teacher made it a particularly bitter pill for some parents to swallow), ultimately forced her resignation. There was no policy within the school or the local authority at the time for dealing with racial incidents at school. No attempt was made to tackle the racial elements of the case by the National Union of Teachers (who acted in defence of their member). Nor was there any attempt by the head master to offer the teacher his support publicly and thus disassociate himself openly from the racial inferences of the alleged complaints.

In all of the above cases there was a demonstrable absence of any policy either in terms of guiding principles, or machinery and resources, for dealing with cases of racial harassment and injustice. None of the responsible bodies, such as the local Council's committees, the trade union or even the service departments themselves (and in this we include the police), had taken any positive steps to redress the impact of racism. No policy statements had been issued, no monitoring procedures for looking into individual cases, or machinery to redress any proven injustice had been established.

The absence of any formal policy was matched in each case by the response of officials discharged with the responsibility of policy

Police racism: the PSI report (1983)

The Policy Studies Institute report on the Metropolitan Police, *Police and People in London*, is undoubtedly the most detailed and extensive study, not just of an individual police force, but of contemporary British policing.

Police attitudes

Racial prejudice and racialist talk are pervasive in the Metropolitan Police, the report found, and some officers appear to cultivate a rhetoric of abuse of black people, a rhetoric encouraged by the norms of working groups. The researchers *never* heard anyone explicitly oppose such talk or make the speaker feel that s/he was boring, speaking out of turn, or erring against unspoken conventions or inhibitions.

Many officers appear to use racialist language among themselves for effect but, the reports say, it is the more casual or automatic use of such language which is the most telling. This was common in conversation, but also commonly used over police radios, even when these could be heard in public places. Several abusive expressions for black people were commonly used:

Hello, she's a nigger. Almost unheard of, a nigger in Esher.

He's very good at parking is Geoff (another policeman). He parked right up a nigger's arse once.

The sooties are giving us a bit of trouble.

The object of these patrols is to protect property, because when these monkeys get through they can cause a great deal of damage . . .

Both the boy and girl that we're going to arrest this morning are spades.

Black people associated with crime

The stopping policy of the police is inseparable from the assumption that black people have committed crimes. It is also related to an assumption made on several specific cases by police that the offender must be black. This was illustrated by a number of cases witnessed by the researchers.

In one case, a bread van had collided with a bicycle ridden by a black man. An inspector told the researcher, 'He was a young West Indian gentleman on the bike, so I presume it's stolen, although he says he got it from a friend.' On another occasion, a detective constable who had gone to a house to investigate a burglary, told the householder: 'I usually associate this type of crime with young blacks. Though, of course, if we catch them it won't be their fault. There'll be all sorts of reasons why they're deprived and why they did it.' On yet another occasion observed, two constables received a message over their personal radios about a robbery. One relayed the description to the other, saying that they were looking for two black youths. A more detailed description over the radio followed shortly after, stating that the youths were white. The constable said, 'I was wrong for once', acknowledging that the first radio description had not mentioned colour. He had simply assumed that only black youths would rob a shop.

What the evidence on stops shows is that there *is* a clear connection between police attitudes and their behaviour towards black people, although it should be emphasised that this is not mentioned in the report's conclusions and summary, and is only noted as a qualification to a general statement about the difference between police attitudes and behaviour. Yet such attitudes and behaviour, as illustrated both by the statistics collected and by incidents observed, show that there is a clear connection in the minds of many police officers between black people and crime. Yet, there is no objective evidence to support such a connection.

Although much has been made of Metropolitan Police statistics purporting to show the disproportionate involvement of black people in crime, particularly street crime, the reality is quite different. A recent analysis of the police statistics by the Home Office itself warned that the statistics had 'limited value as measures of ethnic minority criminality' and warned that it should not be assumed that those types of offences for which ethnic data is available were representative of crime as a whole. More specifically, the Home Office analysis emphasised that while statistics did show the disproportionate involvement of young black people in offences of 'robbery and other violent theft', the ratio of offences to the relevant population age group was still only about 2%, thus indicating that 'no more than a small minority of the non-white population were engaged as assailants in this limited range of offences'. Furthermore, the Home Office cautioned, the factors which explain differences between different ethnic groups range far wider than ethnic appearance, but include a combination of socio-economic factors such as social class, education, employment status and factors relating to social deprivation. Yet, the only variables readily available are those of sex, age and area.

Such words of caution have obviously been lost or gone unnoticed on the police who appear to use the apparent over-involvement of a tiny section of the black population in a tiny proportion of criminal offences (less than 1% of all recorded serious offences) as a justification for seeing a connection between race and crime and for suspecting all young black people.

(*Race and Immigration: The Runnymede Trust Bulletin*, January 1984)

administration. The latter's response in all three cases ranged from indifference to downright hostility. There existed a prevalent view within the bureaucracy that black people are themselves partly to blame for their own situation. They were varyingly accused of being overly sensitive, nuisances, as well as being guilty of the complaints made against them. Overall therefore black people in their attempts to secure redress met with a seemingly inpenetrable wall of inertia and indifference and sometimes institutional victimisation and hostility. Institutional responses such as these are often justified, as we shall see, either by adopting the view that no one group should expect special treatment in the queue for support from public services, or by suggesting that claims made by black people are often exaggerated and sometimes fabricated and thus not worthy of any additional or special policy provision.

Policies and practices which create and maintain racial inequalities

Racism, we suggested in Chapter 1, does not simply operate through policies and practices which have been introduced in direct response to the presence of black people in Britain. Racial inequalities are generated and reproduced through the mere per-

petuation of already existing policies and practices and the construction of policies which take no account of the reality of that
black presence.

Procedures governing recruitment in employment provide some
of the best examples of local institutional racism. For instance,
failure to advertise job vacancies in the black press, vacancies
which are filled as a result of employees' personal contacts ('word
of mouth'), jobs which are filled from within (internal recruitment), recruitment which is restricted to families of employees
('lads and dads' recruitment) and vacancies filled on the basis of
nominations put forward by in-shop trade unions can all effectively
deny access to particular groups outside this network of contacts.
In a recent report into recruitment policies at Unigate Dairies, the
CRE found that word of mouth recruitment had restricted job
opportunities for would-be black milkmen in the West Midlands
including Wolverhampton (CRE 1984a). The firm was not necessarily consciously discriminating in this way; it had merely continued long established recruitment patterns. In both Liverpool
and Wolverhampton the numbers of black employees working for
the local authorities are minimal and certainly well below their
numerical representation in their respective geographical areas. In
Liverpool this situation has been maintained by the sorts of practices referred to above with the result that Liverpool City Council
is about 1000 employees short of a figure which would reflect the
numbers of black people living in the city as a whole (Cf Ben-
Tovim *et al.*, 1980, 1983).

At a one day conference held in 1984, on 'Scarman and After',
the Chief Careers Officer for Wolverhampton was asked how
many black people were employed by the careers department to
which he replied there were none. In excusing this situation
although not condoning it, reference was made to the relatively
low numbers of black people with suitable qualifications who
applied for vacancies when they arose. The barrier of qualifications, which is often used in this way to excuse inequalities,
in turn raises certain questions which need to be directed
at those training institutions (schools, colleges and professional
bodies) responsible for conferring qualifications. The adherence to
rigid patterns of entry to certain jobs via 'O' and 'A' levels, degrees
and/or professional qualifications can and does effectively exclude
disproportionate numbers of black people. Black people are con-

spicuous by their overall absence in Wolverhampton and Liverpool's institutions of higher education; and where they *are* represented, their concentration is in *certain* degree and diploma courses. The introduction of 'access courses' and the positive use of mature entrance which offer alternative routes to higher education and hence to professional qualifications via Liverpool University and Wolverhampton Polytechnic represent two limited attempts to redress those inequalities through restructuring the processes to which they have given rise.

There are many other examples which could be provided here and certainly there is scope for a detailed analysis of this form of institutionalised racism. It is a form of racism which operates almost by default through custom and tradition and the development of policies on the basis of precedence which take no account of the presence of black people. On the rare occasions when some sort of justification for these policies and practices is offered it is generally couched both in the sanctity of tradition, and the commonly held view that to take account of the presence of black people is tantamount to 'special treatment' or 'positive discrimination'.

Policies and practices which abuse the cultural differences of racial minorities

Culture is a term which is incorporated, often inappropriately in our view, into discussion of race relations and racial inequality. It is more often than not used to explain conflict or misunderstanding between groups which arise from differences in custom, religion, manners, dress and language. Although colour is said to heighten these differences it is argued that problems experienced by New Commonwealth immigrants in the post-war period are similar to those faced by Irish and Jewish immigrants in the latter part of the 19th Century. Following this line of analysis racial minorities are thus perceived as *ethnic* minorities and *colour* is one dimension of the broader concept of *ethnicity*.

The tendency to focus on 'ethnic' culture *per se* does serve to shift the emphasis of discussion onto minority groups themselves; the quaint and the exotic as well as the alien and the pathological characteristics of their culture. Predictably and correctly many have come to regard this form of analysis as a diversion from, and by implication an abdication of, institutional responsibilities for inequality. Although we accept the thrust of these criticisms we do believe that it is both possible and necessary to develop a knowledge of culture which neither pathologises the group in question nor eschews the reality of racism. In developing this knowledge we have no interest in exploring 'ethnic' culture for its own sake; for presenting a particular view of black people to a largely white audience. We are only interested in culture insofar as it is amenable to a political analysis. In this sense therefore we are interested in contexts in which cultural differences beg institutional responses and how the failure to respond has helped to create and reinforce racial inequalities. We shall cite some examples below from our own political experience, although in doing so we are not intending to provide a comprehensive survey of all possible institutional manifestations of this form of racism.

Social security provision is one institutional context within which cultural differences and their implications can be identified and explored. For example, during the course of a normal working day the DHSS may well have contact with claimants from the Indian sub-continent. These claimants may wish to make a claim or they may present themselves in order to enquire about their rights to benefits. In both situations they are often-times disadvantaged and/or discriminated against as a result of their cultural difference.

In the first instance the absence of interpreters or DHSS officers who speak the appropriate Asian languages may as a result mean that details of information are inaccurately communicated, or not communicated at all. Individual and family circumstances may be misunderstood by the DHSS officers and/or the criteria for benefit may not be adequately explained to the claimant. Overall, language difficulties often deny access to benefits to which there is legal entitlement.

Assumptions based on particular cultural and ethnic stereotypes are another example of how cultural differences result in unfair treatment. For example it is commonly thought that Asian families provide financial support to their extended families. The result of this is that members of an Asian family, especially young girls and the elderly, are sometimes not informed by the DHSS of their legal entitlement. The irony of this is that when minority group individuals or families *do have* different domestic arrangements, the DHSS often does not treat them seriously.

There are of course, the social security rules themselves which regulate the delivery of benefits. The implicit cultural bias in these rules not only prejudices local DHSS officers but it also can deprive minority groups of their 'safety net' (see above page 49). For example, claimants who wish to make an extended trip to their country of origin do so at the risk of the loss of their right, and their dependants' rights, to income support.

The area of social services provision offers further examples of this particular form of institutional racism, in this case over which the local state has some control. The very essence of social work with its individual casework orientation militates against an understanding and acknowledgement of needs and rights on a group basis. Consequently social patterns within minority groups, which have implications for provision, are often overlooked. The disproportionate number of working women within racial minority groups has implications, for instance, for the geographical location and extent of pre-school provision. The growing population of elderly New Commonwealth people also has implications for provision in terms of type, location and the organisation and facilities offered, for example in meeting the dietary requirements of different groups. The failure to develop policies which respond more directly to those differences has been a matter for considerable concern within Wolverhampton's Council for Community Relations. Although the Social Services Department has recently made extensive applications for Section 11 staff there are indications that equal opportunity policy has not penetrated service delivery. This was made particularly evident when in a major review of existing services, which produced a five year plan, there was minimal reference to racial minorities.

Education too provides further examples of this institutional failure in this respect. It should be noted here that we are not referring to explicit forms of racist stereotyping which appear in fiction and textbooks used in schools and colleges. We would distinguish this more overt form of racism, to which we return below, from the maintenance of policies and practices which ignore the reality of culturally mixed communities when it comes to the planning and organisation of educational institutions.

With respect to the school curricula, for instance, it may not be possible at the present time for schools to make opportunities available for students and pupils to learn *all* of the world's languages. They are, however, in a strong position to respond to the presence of community languages. There are few justifications for excluding Punjabi or Hindi or Chinese from examination sylla-buses, in favour of French, German and Spanish. Yet this is com-monplace, even in areas where community languages are in use and of local importance. For example in 1984 in Wolverhampton, only three of the town's secondary schools offered any of the three major Asian languages. In terms of effects the absence of these Asian languages maintains the idea that they (and perhaps their speakers) are less important than the existing languages on offer. In some cases it also denies mother-tongue speakers of community languages the one opportunity they have to take advantage of their linguistic inheritance for the purpose of school performance. This is in contrast with many white indigenous children, who have lan-guage 'on their side' for most of the exams they sit or subjects they study.

There are many more examples of how our schools, colleges, and polytechnics fail as institutions to be sensitive to culture and therefore effectively make educational access and opportunity comparatively more competitive and restricted for racial minority groups than for the 'white' indigenous. In addition to the way processes and procedures *fail to take* account of language, values, traditions and customs, these disadvantages also arise as a result of steps these institutions *do take*.

We can best exemplify this by referring to a recent educational development in Wolverhampton. Since the early 1980s the LEA has provided some financial assistance and support for voluntary-attended Asian language classes on Saturdays. This initiative was the result of community pressures dating back to the mid 1970s. In part these classes are seen as a concession by the LEA to local demands, but the community also recognises the fact that the LEA has failed to make any substantial changes to mainstream educa-tional provision. There is a strong feeling that the LEA has used the Saturday classes in order to be seen to 'be multicultural' rather than because it has made a serious commitment to ensure cultural plurality and equal oportunity for its educational users.

Our final example in this section comes from the area of youth provision. The provision of leisure and recreational facilities for Asian girls however is particularly relevant to our present argu-ment, since their take-up of statutory youth service provision in

Wolverhampton is minimal and probably closer to non-existent. Various reasons have been put forward to explain their absence from the town's youth facilities: the absence of segregated (girls only) provision; transport difficulties and finally lack of any contact between officers, administrators and youth leaders and the Asian community. Despite the explicit identification of these reasons with their clear implications for policy and practice, the youth service has continually failed to develop a positive policy to meet the needs of this group of young people. Once again this is an area of policy under local control, since the loosely defined framework provided under the 1944 Education Act leaves considerable scope for local initiatives.

Policies and practices which assume negative racial stereotypes

We conclude our discussion of policy with one final form of institutionalised racism, not because we regard it as any less important than the others but because traditionally it receives more attention perhaps than the other three. Negative stereotyping is used here to refer to a patterned understanding of black people in which the latter are attributed negative characteristics. The process of stereotyping in policy formulation and administration can thus be linked to the adoption of certain ideas and perspectives discussed in Chapter 1. One example for instance is the assumption underpinning one side of the race – intelligence debate which attributes inferior mental capacities to black people. Another is the assumption that Afro-Caribbean and Asian cultural patterns are somehow deviations and hence inferior to the Western cultural model. This in turn may then be linked to the view that black people themselves are responsible for the conditions of inequality reviewed in the first part of this chapter.

There are numerous examples from our own organisational work of the kinds of practices experienced daily by black people in their contact with local institutions. Consider for instance those negative assumptions regarding black people which have underpinned the following administrative decisions: teachers in their assessment of the intellectual potential of pupils when it comes to streaming and the submission of names for examination entrance; teachers again, in their assessment of disruptive behaviour and decisions to withdraw children from normal classes; employers in their decisions to recruit black people on the basis of their assumed aptitude for work as well as ability to do the job; magistrates when it comes to deciding whether a black offender is suitable for probation or should receive a custodial sentence; housing visitors when it comes to interpreting housing standards and family needs; police officers when it comes to stopping, searching and detaining young black people on the street; and finally, although by no means exhaustively, social security officers when it comes to the verification of personal circumstances prior to the approval of a claim.

We are not talking about one-off cases in the above examples or cases of individual racism. The set of negative stereotypical assumptions which enter into administrative practice represent an integral part of the culture of numerous professional groups. In other words these negative assumptions form part of the professional's view of her/his public, thus providing the means by which certain patterned responses are rendered acceptable and intelligible when it comes to dealing with black people. To a large extent, in our view, the degree of discretion afforded to officials in the above cases results from the absence of policies and practices which are designed explicitly and unambiguously to redress racial inequalities. In other words this particular form of institutionalised racism is exacerbated by the other three.

In our experience we have encountered few local policies, as opposed to practices, which have been constructed explicitly on the basis of negative stereotyping. Policing policies however do provide one example. Policy decisions to deploy resources in particular areas of the inter city, the use of special task groups for particular aspects of policing, the use of beat officers and the promotion of community policing have all been premissed on certain negative assumptions regarding black criminality. In doing so they make certain judgements about the significance and gravity of suspected black crime vis-a-vis other kinds of suspected crime. The introduction of liaison committees and attempts to secure co-operation of local leaders to 'police' their own communities is entirely consistent with these assumptions, so that recent attempts to approach the problem of black crime via liaison and co-operation nevertheless retain the original conception of the problem, and hence the negative assumptions which underpin it.

Conclusions

In the first part of this chapter we reaffirmed what is essentially the starting point of our work, on which this book is based: the existence of very real inequalities of conditions between black and white in post-war Britain. Moreover, we found that public policy, far from redressing these inequalities, has invariably served to reinforce existing inequalities and at times create new ones of its own. We examined the role of local policy in particular in the second part of this chapter drawing on case study material from our own political experience. What this leads to is a quite complex set of processes at work within the context of any one institutional setting in which policy and administrative practice articulate with 'external' conditions which themselves become part of the cultural and administrative fabric of the institution itself.

Statistical and case study evidence of inequalities can be analysed in terms of a process of policy making and administrative practice. The maintenance of certain policies, the absence of others, the pursuit of certain practices, the resistance to others, can be located more precisely in terms of the workings of the institution and can be seen to be instrumental in direct and indirect terms in the resulting inequalities. An educational policy of no curriculum change (including no explicit policy on combating racism in schools), a housing policy which excludes monitoring, a youth policy which stresses integrated provision, an employment policy which operates on a word of mouth basis, all of which can indirectly discriminate against black people, are all traceable to institutional processes which embrace policy formulation and instigation on the one hand and implementation and administrative practice on the other.

Within these processes the exercise of power is a major force. Institutional power is in part conferred by government through legislation, policy and the releasing of resources for institutional use and provision. Internally, however, it may depend on policies, rules and procedures which have evolved through practice, some of which are written, others not, but all of which vary in their degree of enforcement and the scope that they provide for individual exercise of power above and beyond that formally prescribed. Of course this residue of power is not itself unlimited. There are limits even to the exercise of discretionary administrative power for example, the withholding of information, the denial of rights and the withdrawal of facilities and services. A knowledge of those conditions which underpin the realisation of power as well as its limits is an important precondition for effective anti-racist struggles.

Racial ideologies of varying forms have clearly permeated institutional processes. They may take the form of institutional resistance to the reality of discrimination and inequality, or resistance to the notion that those from different cultures should be treated any differently or 'favourably'. Alternatively, these ideologies are realised through a lack of awareness of the effects of certain policies or practices vis-a-vis access to and provision of services for multi-racial groups, or at the other extreme, and perhaps not as unrelated as it might appear, the conscious and explicit use of negative racial stereotypes in policy formulation and administrative practice. Although these ideologies do not originate within the institution itself they have become an integral part of the traditions and mores of institutional practice and invariably take on particular forms peculiar to individual institutional settings.

The framework for the analysis of institutionalised racism should not be regarded as a basis for the reconstruction of a static set of conditions. On the contrary the processes identified in this chapter are contingent on forces and conditions which are subject to change from a variety of sources and in a variety of directions. In what follows we shall examine struggles for institutional change from the standpoint of local organisations. In doing so we shall develop our analysis of institutional processes undertaken in this chapter. We shall be 'testing' the various forces of resistance and positive change through our own experience of the political, including campaign interventions. The 'positive' outcome of these struggles and the role of central policy initiatives in these changes are the focus of Chapters 5 and 6. Overall the contingency of the outcome will become increasingly evident although not before the marked disparities in access to and exercise of institutional power are seen to have left their mark on struggles between contending forces and their subsequent outcomes measured in ways documented and reviewed in the course of this chapter.

4 Local Organisations and Racial Equality

The overall significance of organisations in the struggle for racial equality can be understood in three ways in the context of this book. In the first instance, organisations, whatever their specific characteristics, provide forums for the identification of commonly acknowledged problems and the articulation of collective demands. They can thus serve as an important antidote to those atomising tendencies at work within representative democracies. These tendencies serve to limit a person's political role to voting, and in the last resort, to seeking redress on an individual basis (e.g. complaints to councillors and MPs). Individual complaints and votes, however provide no real opportunity to tackle institutional racism. Local organisations, on the other hand, allow for discussion and action on important and specific race-related issues.

We have already discussed, in previous chapters, the role of policy, both national and local, in producing and reproducing racial inequality. It is therefore not surprising that policies as well as institutional practices are key reference points for local race-related organisations. Sometimes determination to change existing policy is the driving force of the organisation; at other times the organisation's activities are an attempt to overcome the inadequacies of policy. Policy is also sometimes the 'enabler' – that is, the organisation uses it to create new opportunities. This integral link with policy, then, is a further dimension to an analysis of race-related organisations in local politics.

Thirdly, despite their different priorities and strategies, organisations committed to racial equality suffer in varying degrees from marginalisation, a term we shall consider more fully in the next chapter. In the case of local organisations it pushes them out on to the periphery of local politics. In so doing it serves to restrict local debate and struggle to those policies which most visibly affect racial groups, for example Section 11 or Inner City Policy. As a result those areas of policy and those institutions at the heart of our local cultural life, such as education, employment and housing, escape close scrutiny. Local organisations are therefore limited in the attack they can make on institutional racism.

Moreover, marginalisation limits the options open to local race organisations both in terms of their development of strategies and the formulation of demands. Theirs is a struggle against exclusion, which entails manoeuvering a position for themselves away from the periphery and towards the centre of mainstream politics. Not surprisingly their demands often call for revolutionary changes, at revolutionary speeds. At the other extreme, they sometimes are unwilling or unable to articulate their demands. Marginalisation of organisations must then be a crucial factor in any analysis of local policy and politics.

In the course of this chapter, we shall discuss three kinds of organisations whose dominant forms of practice are different from one another, although they are all essentially committed to the elimination of racial inequalities. We define and categorise these three types of organisation here according to their dominant form of practice as well as by their political reputation. They include anti-racist organisations; community and project organisations for Afro-Caribbean, Asian and/or multiracial groups; and race relations pressure groups. Individually we have had varying degrees of experience of all three kinds of organisations, including some whose activities are not confined exclusively to one form of practice. The bulk of our political involvement has been through our respective Community Relations Councils, and additionally in Wolverhampton through the local Labour Party (we include both of these in the third of the categories we have identified above – race relations pressure groups). There are reasons for this and these will serve to justify our extensive treatment of both organisations in the latter part of this chapter.

A framework for analysing local organisations

Anti-racist organisations

Although we would argue that all organisations in which we have participated have put forward alternative priorities and strategies for combating racism, and are therefore anti-racist, we are referring here to a particular kind of organisation which emerged in the 1970s in response to the activities and growing popularity of the National Front and the far Right. The two with which we had particular contact (two of our group were secretaries of their respective organisations) were the Merseyside Anti-Racialist Alliance (MARA) and the Wolverhampton Anti-Racist Committee (WARC). Both have subsequently lapsed with many individual activists moving away from the area or across into other organisations including local community relations councils. The two organisations offered some interesting points of contrast as well as other more predictable points of similarity and convergence.

The base of support for WARC for instance was much narrower than MARA. The Wolverhampton group was made up of activists who came primarily from ultra-left groupings centred around the local polytechnic's Student Union, notably from the International Marxist Group and to a lesser extent, the Socialist Workers Party. Members of the group from the Labour party were often, although not exclusively, also members of the IMG. The membership of the committee did expand at certain moments, most notably around the time of the street conflicts in 1978 when it attracted support from Wolverhampton's young black community for a period of several weeks. This apart, the group was largely isolated from local black organisations with the exception of the Indian Workers Association (GB) and in particular through the active involvement of the then national president. In the main the activists of the group focused on racism's most repressive and unjust manifestations, that is to say, the extreme right, immigration control and the police. Demonstrations, counter marches, leafletting, deportation cases became the hallmark of organisational practice although the Committee did organise a conference on education and were instrumental in the creating of a set of joint working parties on primary and secondary school curriculum and language. The Committee developed a life of its own through its tactics which encouraged a syndrome of demonstrations. At these demonstrations there were police arrests which provided further opportunities for anti-police activity, more demonstrations and more arrests. This pursuit of direct action couched in the characteristic rhetoric of the far left and forcefully argued at Sunday afternoon meetings guaranteed a low level of participation. In this kind of political environment the reality of mass non-involvement in the Committee appeared less of a concern to active members than the need to challenge any deviation on the part of 'faint-hearted' members on questions concerned with participation, tactics and organisational activities.

In contrast MARA attracted a broader base of support, thanks partly perhaps to the existence of a local Anti-Nazi League group which attracted, as it did elsewhere, a dominant contingent of active support from organisations of the far left. Although MARA responded to the activities of the far right, it operated in the main with a much broader conception of racism and its complex institutional forms. This was reflected in a variety of local campaigns, on the media, health, education as well as the issue of equal opportunity in the local authority. The organisation took advantage of its broader membership in the pursuit of positive initiatives as well as negative protest and opposition campaigns. Hence MARA's links with the media proved significant in the creation of slots on both press and radio for the promotion of anti-racism. Similarly direct links with the local Trades Council led to developments on equal opportunity, an achievement we shall discuss more fully in the next chapter.

The ultimate demise of both organisations was in part due to their exclusive reliance on voluntary commitment, the waning electoral fortunes of the extreme right, and the emergence of the CRCs in both Wolverhampton and Liverpool as possible forums for the pursuit of anti-racist objectives. Whilst MARA did make certain limited tangible gains during its lifetime, neither organisation can be said to have mounted what could be regarded as a serious challenge to racism even in the narrow sense in which the term was used within WARC. The state remained successfully intact, diffusing protest as well as deflecting and ridiculing attempts to challenge its authority. WARC remained marginal, its members cast as fanatics, its demands rejected as extreme and its tactics equated with those of the far right. This came as no surprise to the core of active members of WARC. Their political stance assumed continuing defeat in the absence of mass insurrection. The realisation of the latter thus played an integral, although sometimes unstated, role in the formulation of strategy. It was this 'all or nothing' stance which, in terms of WARC's own organisational objectives, arguably ended in nothing. A more accurate assessment, however, would need to take account of the less tangible, more indirect effects of high profile anti-racist activity. Certainly local extreme right wing organisations suffered electoral setbacks in the late 1970s and early 1980s, the credit for which could in part be attributed to the successful anti-racist campaigns, local and national, which linked the extreme right with fascism and Nazism.

In the successful pursuit of their political targets, anti-racist organisations may well have helped to martyr themselves as the police, politicians and the media increasingly equated the activities of the left and right. Perhaps more significant, however, was the longer term impact on subsequent struggles for racial equality. Racism itself has become more widely used and acknowledged even in official documents. Local officials and politicians have begun to use the term themselves although it is generally restricted to individuals and not conceded in institutional terms. Nevertheless, any form of official acknowledgement of the reality of racism is a significant gain and one in which anti-racist organisations, certainly in Liverpool and Wolverhampton, played an important role.

Community and project groups (for Afro-Caribbean, Asian and/or multi-racial groups)

Community and project work is carried out in a number of organisational contexts including black self-help projects and associations, supplementary schools and welfare organisations. These organisations vary in terms of their composition of staff and management, and their overall priorities and activities – for example providing welfare rights advice, leisure facilities, refuge, language support or training in literacy and numeracy. They do, however, share what is a relatively strong position, in comparison with other kinds of 'race' organisation, in their opportunity to establish a more credible and sometimes secure niche within the local state. There are several reasons for the respectability these types of community organisation attract, and these reasons simultaneously help to explain our own limited involvement in this form of organisational activity. First and most important supplementary schools, youth club facilities and welfare rights projects, do not in themselves challenge institutional policy and practice. In the main these initiatives seek to supplement existing provision, rather than to change it directly, any challenge being implicit. Secondly there are acknowledged and accepted channels for establishing and developing such organisations: seeking grant aid from local authorities or charitable trust, locating and leasing premises, attracting would-be users of the provision, are all pursued on the basis of well established procedures. In the main, alternative forms of pressure, such as the more 'extreme' forms associated with anti-racism, are either considered superfluous or are beyond the political will of the organisation. Thirdly this consensus over relationships with outside bodies is mirrored internally. Projects and self-help groups operate, if not a closed membership, one that is certainly more restricted and less accountable than other kinds of organisation in our experience. Internal conflict within the organisation is thus minimised as self appointed management committees exercise control over their own membership as well as staff appointments. Fourthly the more limited objectives of this kind of organisation act as a further check on potential areas of disagreement and consequently enhance the standing of the organisation, albeit on somewhat superficial grounds, in the eyes of the external community.

In some ways the objectives, strategies and day-to-day activities of community-style organisations complement those of the local state extremely well. Some kind of provision is made for the black community and the state can be seen to be playing a supporting role, through for example funding. Rather than challenging institutional provision and practice as a whole, these initiatives sit quite comfortably alongside it. Their effects will, in the main, be immediate but at the same time restricted to users of their provision, rather than extending beyond this and having wider ramifications. Moreover the closed character of these organisations is well suited to the closed door style of negotiation and political bargaining prevalent in certain areas of local authority practice. Ironically, therefore, despite their relative inaccessibility and lack of accountability, such organisations often come to be regarded by local authorities as more authentic mouthpieces of the community, and, in so doing, are played off against other more open kinds of organisation.

Policy-related, campaigning organisations

In many respects both of the above kinds of organisation, the anti-racist, and the community and project work organisations, stand at opposite ends of the organisational spectrum to one another. They do share, however, a certain conception of politics which makes a distinction between 'doing' and 'talking'. For anti-racist organisations 'doing' is demonstrating on the street, organising mass leafletting or counter-marches. For community and project work organisations 'doing' is coming into direct contact with black people and meeting their needs on an immediate face-to-face basis. One corollary of this distinction is a shared opposition to and suspicion of talking and writing which is aimed at medium and long-term change. Amongst both kinds of organisation there is therefore a tendency to delegitimise the third kind of organisational activity which campaigns for positive policy change on an institutional basis. In considering this third kind of organisation we shall focus on the local Labour Party and Community Relations Councils, since these are where our political efforts have in the main been concentrated.

Our involvement in these organisations can be justified on three grounds. First they have a structure which ensures that their leaders and officers are accountable to their membership on a formal democratic basis. However 'unrepresentative' these organisations might appear, there is a potential openness and accessibility which is absent in the main from community style organisations and from anti-racist organisations. Secondly they seek to challenge racism on a broad institutional basis, establishing connections between policy and practice on the one hand and racial inequalities on the other. They do not, in the main, restrict racism to its most extreme manifestations, to individual pathology, nor do they set out to provide substitute or supplementary forms of provision without tackling the policy framework within which provision is made or not made. Finally they have the resources and links with national bodies which not only facilitate continuity and sustained campaign and pressure group activity, but also enable the development of issues on a wider basis, and the support of various kinds from national bodies.

In developing a more detailed assessment of the role of both CRC's and the Labour Party, we shall critically assess their role not only in terms of their external pressure group activities but also in terms of their internal workings. In both cases we have been actively involved not only in attempts to campaign externally for racial equality but also to provide a more effective organisational base in order to do so.

Local Labour Parties

Our commitment to the Labour Party is integrally bound up with our commitment to socialism, so that for us the struggle for racial equality is part of a broader struggle for the realisation of socialist principles. Loosely these entail the redistribution of wealth, which penalises neither race nor class; the creation of democratic institutional forms which increase popular, including minority, participation and control and the promotion of a morality which serves to legitimate and support these principles at the expense of a morality which rests on the pursuit of self-interest and competition and with it the inevitable legitimation of inequality and injustice. For all its shortcomings, some of which we consider below, the Labour Party has a base of support, a philosophy, as well as access to the formal apparatus of the state which together offer the most realistic prospect for pursuing the struggle for socialism and racial equality within the context of British party politics.

Despite the above comments our commitment to the Labour Party is by no means unreserved or unqualified. The Party has no God-given monopoly over socialism or racial equality, nor is it immune to influences and conditions which militate against the realisation of those principles. As critics and sceptics have rightly argued, current immigration policies and processes owe as much to post-war Labour governments as they do to Conservative governments, past and present. Immigration, however, is not the only yardstick against which the Party as a whole should be assessed, however convenient it might be for those wishing to develop an argument whose logic links the Labour Party with social democracy, social democracy with capitalism and capitalism with racism. The consensus on immigration control between Conservative and

Labour governments cannot be attributed to the Labour Party as a whole, nor can it be used to lump together all post-war policy initiatives on race regardless of their party of origin. It is no coincidence for instance that the Labour Party has been responsible for all three Race Relations Acts in 1965, 1968 and 1976. Linked to these, although not always translated into legislative initiatives, have been a series of reports, discussion papers, policy statements all of which have made explicit in varying degrees the problems of racism, racial disadvantage and special needs, and most of which have been instigated or produced by past Labour administrations. The White Papers *Racial Discrimination* (Home Office, 1975) and *The West Indian Community* (Home Office, 1978a), The Green Paper *Education in Schools* (DES, 1977), *Education for all* (DES, 1985) the consultative document outlining proposals for replacing Section 11 (Home Office, 1978b) and the Thompson Report on the Youth Service (DES, 1982) are all examples of Labour-inspired initiatives. The work of the party's Race Action Group is important to mention in this respect. Established in 1979, it has worked closely with prominent London based councillors and some Labour politicians in producing newsletters, reports, for instance on monitoring and multicultural education and race manifestos, and it has been involved in seeking to develop more direct forms of black participation in the Party through the establishment of Black Sections.

What follows however focuses exclusively at a local level and in particular on the two local Labour Parties in Liverpool and Wolverhampton. Although both parties emerge from our assessment apparently successfully our analysis demonstrates that this is only superficial. Behind the success lies rhetoric, posturing and piecemeal concessions which betray a deep-seated resistance to the development of anti-racist policies. These can in part be attributed to local political ideologies and in part to local party structures and the democratic framework or absence of it, within which party policy emerges.

Local Labour parties in both Wolverhampton and Liverpool increased their overall majority of seats at the most recent local elections (1984). In Wolverhampton the majority increased to eleven to ensure continuous Labour control of the town for 15 years by the time of the next local elections in 1986. The Labour Party in Liverpool too increased its majority to seventeen in the May 1984 elections, a result which was interpreted by the Labour leadership as an endorsement of the Party's proposed illegal budget. Its history at least in electoral terms has been much more chequered and its position until recently less secure than the Wolverhampton Labour Group. In fact it has only been in control since 1983 prior to which Liverpool's council had, for a number of years been dominated by the Liberals with Conservative support.

Although Liverpool's Labour Group only gained control of the city council in 1983 it has, albeit reluctantly and inconsistently, supported several measures aimed at redressing racial inequality. The Labour Group (that is the group of Labour councillors on the city council) have both accepted in principle the creation of a race relations unit and race relations sub-committee and proceeded to appoint a principal race relations advisor. It has also agreed to apply for S11 funding for staff for the Multiracial Education Unit, the local black access course to higher education and for a Chinese unit within the Social Services Department. It has also prepared a code of practice on racist incidents in schools and colleges, and supported the Liverpool 8 Law Centre, as well as other community projects.

Similarly, in Wolverhampton, the Labour Group can take the credit for a number of recent initiatives during its period of control on the council. Amongst these have been the introduction of an equal opportunity policy; the creation of a race relations committee, a full committee of the council, with representatives from Afro-Caribbean and Asian communities and serviced by a complement of full-time race relations advisers. Furthermore it has expanded the staff and responsibilities of the Multi-Cultural Education Service, introduced the teaching of mother-tongues into a number of its secondary schools and developed in-service training courses for its head teachers. It has funded an Afro-Caribbean Cultural Centre, a Sikh temple and premises for the WRPA (Wolverhampton Rastafarian Progressive Association). The Housing Department has kept ethnic records for a number of years and has appointed a liaison officer with responsibilities for ethnic minorities. It has appointed specialist staff to work in the library service and claimed on average over two million pound per annum for the last 19 years under S11 of the Local Government Act 1966. It has appointed four full-time youth workers of Afro-Caribbean descent and a research worker in social services with a race relations brief.

The above initiatives, however, must be set against a background of widespread resistance on the part of both Labour groups to other and more far-reaching kinds of reform. Furthermore the initiatives themselves are not always what they appear, often reflecting a less than full commitment to racial equality and its policy implications. In Liverpool, for instance, the appointment of the race relations advisor must be examined against a history of failure to provide financial or political support to the various initiatives agreed by the Race Relations Liaison Committee. Amongst these were: the refusal to set up a working party on racial harassment on council estates or to support a training scheme for housing managers, the continued opposition to monitoring, the failure to implement a number of S11 initiatives agreed by the Home Office and finally rejection of the principle of separate provision with respect to a sheltered housing scheme for the black elderly, which had already received support from the Department of the Environment. The need to break down this resistance was not assisted by the appointment of the Chairperson of the Race Relations Sub-Committee or the Adviser, both of whom had no prior experience or expertise in race issues. The fact that the Race Relations Sub-Committee was later abolished gives evidence to the fact that these appointments enabled the Labour Group to maintain its political control over the black community.

In Wolverhampton the main official forum for debating race issues is the Race Relations and Equal Opportunities Committee. Although it has the status of a full committee of the council, a number of factors serve to undermine its potential impact. Firstly its remit covers not only race relations but issues concerning women and the disabled. Although all three areas can be loosely linked to the principle of equal opportunity, inequalities with regard to each, as we have argued, are quite specific and hence demand correspondingly specific kinds of policy response. Furthermore despite its full status, the Committee has no budget and no directorate and until 1985 a staff of one, the Race Relations Adviser, to serve it. It is not surprising therefore that the borough's equal opportunity policy which has been in existence since 1981 has yet to be used as a strategic instrument in the promotion of equal employment opportunities for Wolverhampton's Afro-Caribbean and Asian Communities or as a basis for monitoring its own mainstream service provision.

Despite its widely publicised initiative on keeping records in the housing department, little attempt has been made by Labour's controlling group to use these records directly to provide the basis for redressing known inequalities. One such inequality, a direct consequence of the points system, on which offers of council properties are made, has resulted in the concentration of young black single people in the least desirable high rise accommodation. What initiatives have been taken in the field of housing have come from within the housing department (e.g. a policy document on racial harassment) rather than from political pressure from the Labour Group.

S11 funding has a story of its own which is told more fully in Chapter 6. Nevertheless, the availability of that grant did provide the local Labour group with an opportunity to develop policies specifically designed to promote racial equality. Moreover the grant could have been used as an opportunity to create forums for black participation in policy development. The Labour group attempted neither. Instead it adhered to the ambiguous letter of the original policy statement. Even when it was forced to create consultation procedures with minority communities by virtue of administrative changes laid down by central government in 1984, it only capitulated under pressure from the community, and even then according to its own limited definition of consultation.

In the area of youth provision the appointment of four full-time youth workers and the funding of a research study must be considered in the context of wide ranging recommendations which date back at least to 1977, the first Wolverhampton Council for Community Relations report on youth. The implementation of these recommendations would have restructured the local youth service and increased representation of young people from minority groups in policy-making arenas of the council as well as made provision for groups of young people, male and female, from Afro-Caribbean and Asian communities.

Sources of resistance: class-oriented ideologies

The significance of the Militant tendency within Liverpool's Labour Party cannot be overestimated. In terms of its contribution

to the struggle for racial equality it has created formidable obstacles which local organisations have been forced to confront and
overcome. Despite our general commitment to the Labour party,
which has already been acknowledged in this chapter, it has to be
admitted that in Liverpool, where positive initiatives have been
taken, this has largely been in spite of, and not thanks to, its local
Labour Party. The latter's resistance to such initiatives is bound up
with Militant's view of the world. It is a world in which any align-
ment with positive race policies would only serve to divert and
divide Liverpool's working class community from its historic mis-
sion: the realisation of socialism through class struggle. At the
heart of its conception of socialism is public ownership and control
from the centre. Its avowed opposition to racism is sustained without any serious attempt to eradicate it through positive policy and
political intervention.

Similarly, in Wolverhampton there is a tendency within the
Labour Group which, although not Militant, it not dissimilar in
terms of its effects to those of Liverpool's Labour Group. It has its
roots in the Black Country's predominantly white male trade
union and Labour movement. Since the onset of the recession, the
Group has become increasingly responsive to the withdrawal of
capital from the region, industrial restructuring and job losses,
particularly in the manufacturing sector and sensitive about the
emergence of new sources of labour from the post-war period
onwards, both female on the one hand and New Commonwealth
on the other. This has given rise to a strongly protective and
parochial outlook that has fostered a colour-blindness which,
along with a class orientation to public policy and provision, at
times manifests itself in more overt forms of intolerance and hostility.

Sources of resistance: policy-making and local democracy

Our discussion of local Labour parties so far has focused on local
policy and local political ideologies prevalent within the two controlling groups in Liverpool and Wolverhampton. Our emphasis
on the higher echelons of the two local parties will be of little
surprise to local branch and constituency activists. It is a reflection
of the lack of involvement of the lower echelons of the party in
policy development. In fact although there is little evidence of

grass-roots support for positive initiatives on race, those initiatives that have been taken from below have failed to penetrate the labyrinthine party machine.

The relative absence of policy deliberations is a reflection of the party's local structure and the role played by the local party leadership. Most ordinary party members seeking to influence council policy do so by putting forward a resolution to their local branch. So long as it receives the support of the majority of the membership present, it will reach the Labour Group only after it has passed through and won the support of the General Committee of the constituency and then the District Party. District Party is the policy-making body of the local Labour party, its links being with the local Labour Group on the council rather than with the Party at a national level. The District Party's links with rank and file members of the party are made via constituency general committees as well as directly with branches through delegate representation. This cumbersome procedure often means that by the time the process is complete, the resolutions are invariably superseded by events or preempted by decisions already acted upon. Although District Party and its officers have become popular targets for grass roots criticism, the problems are not peculiar to that body but lie in the mechanisms and structures within the party as a whole for policy formulations and decisions.

The 'resolution' is an extremely crude and blunt instrument for policy innovation. It allows for a principle of policy to be divorced from the context in which it is to be acted upon. The failure of resolutions which have successfully worked their way up through the party apparatus is invariably seen to be the result of conservatism, incompetence or a betrayal by local party leadership. In our view, changes in party policy will require more than a change in leadership. They require, from their formulation onwards, a form of calculation which takes account of the context within which their underpinning principles might be implemented. In the main such principles can only be specified in the context of much fuller documentation and analysis and the involvement of party members.

It was against a background of frustration and concern arising from the problems identified above, that Wolverhampton's South West Constituency Party established a series of policy groups in the early part of 1980. The overriding purpose of these groups was to attempt to co-ordinate the fragmentary interventions such as public meetings, petitions, resolutions, branch discussions and to respond to single policy issues like education, human rights, social policy, race relations, economic strategy, housing, women, thereby providing the possibility of a more coherent approach to policy development within the party.

The policy groups developed very unevenly and have since all but ceased to function. During their period of activity some sought to organise their activities around public meetings and resolutions. The human rights and economic strategy groups developed in this way. Some organised their activities around campaign work, often based around week-long programmes organised by national organisations including the Labour party. The housing and women's groups both developed on this basis. The race relations group, in contrast, worked towards the production of policy documents. The two principal documents produced during the 1980–82 period, on youth policy and education (Wolverhampton South West Constituency Labour Party 1981, 1982), have been directed towards the local Labour group on the one hand, and used a basis for branch and constituency discussion on the other. In practice although the policy group sought to use formal party machinery to press for policy change within the borough, more effective links were established with members of the Labour group through informal contacts. We shall return to this below. Variations in terms of the constituency policy groups might be explained in part in terms of the experience, background and membership of the groups, the varying significance attached to specific forms of intervention and the nature of the policy area around which the groups were formed.

There are a number of factors however which overall have clearly limited the impact of the policy groups on local policy development. The first concerns the relationship between the policy groups and existing party machinery. It has already been suggested that resolutions are not the most effective means for the development of policy within the party. At the same time, it must be said they are ideally suited to existing party structures. A resolution, tacked on to the end of a business meeting and passed without discussion, can thus serve to convince the more sceptical elements of the party membership that the party is, after all, about politics. Moreover while the principle of anti-racism may be comfortably and safely contained within a resolution, intra-party conflicts are more likely to emerge in the rare event of a detailed discussion which necessarily explores the origin and forms of racism and unequal opportunity in more depth. For example, in the case of constituency and branch discussions of the Race Relations Policy Group's youth document, a variety of positions did indeed emerge. As well as some general support for its proposals, there were negative responses based on the refusal to separate out the needs of young black people from youth in general, and there were even protests of an overtly racist nature. Their emergence thus prevented the establishment of a consensus and a failure to agree on channels for pursuing further the issues contained in the document.

This problem of the 'resolution', in a general sense, is exacerbated through the existence of two tiers, Constituency and District Party, through which documents have to pass before being potentially available for discussion in Labour groups. The eventual demise of the constituency policy groups was thus at the time more than compensated for by the establishment of such groups within the machinery of District Party in 1982. The opportunities for establishing more direct links with Labour Group through District Party seemed at the time to increase their scope for impact. The groups, made up of representatives from each of Wolverhampton's three constituencies, did meet regularly and did produce reports and submissions, which were submitted to a conference of the District Party. The reports were intended to provide the basis for submission to the local party manifesto. The conference was eventually held in 1983. Only a couple of dozen delegates attended, reports were discussed but no decisions were taken. The handful of members of Labour Group present raised a number of objections to the proposals from the equal opportunity group on race and women and made no committment in principle to the papers under discussion.

The survival of the policy groups owes as much to the perseverence and commitment of party activists as to any success they might have had in influencing policy formulation within the party. Their future, given present conditions, is likely to be dominated by periods of low, at times dormant membership and inconclusive discussion. There has been a growing tendency since 1983 to promote council based forums for policy-making through the establishment of working parties such as those on the grand Theatre and animal rights, the proliferation of sub-committees for example on women, the disabled and race relations, and ad hoc research initiatives such as the youth review. Such initiatives serve to centralise rather than democratise responsibility for policy development within the party through the creation of corporate blocs within the authority comprising politicians, officers and co-opted members appointed largely at the discretion of the Labour Group. The reinforcement of divisions between the civic centre and the local Labour Party as a whole effectively weaken the already tenuous links between them.

Grassroots participation in policy-making within the party, of which policy groups are one example, rely on receptive and responsive party leadership. Indeed responsibility for Wolverhampton's introduction of an equal opportunity policy rests with a coterie of the party leadership. In this respect the local party as a whole can play a significant role in policy development although only at the pleasure of the leadership itself. The maintenance of informal structures have to some extent reinforced certain oligarchical tendencies within the party in both Liverpool and Wolverhampton. Policy groups and other would-be participatory mechanisms have thus been largely bypassed. As a result participation operates almost through patronage rather than the enforcement of structures of accountability which are binding on leadership.

Summary

In summary then whilst the organisational structure, the broad ideological commitment to socialism, and access to the political system make the Labour Party a significant instrument for positive change, its role in both Wolverhampton and Liverpool has been limited. In Liverpool the dominant Militant faction have with a very few exceptions effectively confined anti-racism to a slogan. In Wolverhampton there exist a range of somewhat superficial but nonetheless positive initiatives behind which a number of more profound problems have been uncovered. The resistance to attempts to develop more wide-ranging and sustained policy interventions is not merely a reflection of a lack of commitment in terms of racism, nor is it just a reflection of the absence of mandatory participatory mechanisms within the party. The resistance is in part a reflection of the absence of any clear conception of socialist policy and its implications for the local state.

As local Labour parties, amidst a set of formidable international and national constraints, not to mention pressure from local ratepayers, begin to translate a fairly narrow abstract set of ideals into local practice, a few limited courses of action emerge. The practice of opposing all policy initiatives in principle rather than seeking to promote viable policy alternatives is one such course. This political tendency is sometimes referred to as oppositionism. Another kind of response entails the indiscriminate support for all things public, which in Liverpool has led to opposition to non-municipal forms of ownership and control such as housing co-operatives, as well as hostility to voluntary sector initiatives and to the decentralisation of services and community participation in their delivery. The politics of discretion, involving informal deals and ad hoc forms of participation is another. All three can of course be pursued together despite the inconsistencies that this sometimes implies. The failure to understand the nature and scope of local policy for socialist advance has limited the impact of Labour parties in both geographical areas. The nature of the development of positive policies on race within the Labour party must be understood, therefore, in the context of what amounts to a set of ideological, organisational and political constraints.

Community relations councils

Our active commitment to and involvement in community relations councils in Liverpool (MCRC) and Wolverhampton (WCCR) can be linked to three aspects of their philosophy and organisation. Other local organisations share one or at most two of these characteristics but rarely combine all three. The first relates to the philosophies of MCRC and WCCR, both of which contain an explicit commitment to racial equality and the combating of institutional racism. Next, and despite the conflicts which are inevitably provoked through the pursuit of these objectives, both CRCs nevertheless attract funding which gives them the capacity to survive. In addition to their philosophy and financial security there can be added finally, the openness and heterogeneity of their membership. Local CRCs as umbrella organisations play a co-ordinating role in the community. They thus encourage the affiliation of local organisations and groups rather than limiting new membership either formally through their constitution or informally through the selection or appointment of their members on an ad hoc basis. As a result CRCs are not only open but have the potential to develop a broad-based platform both in composition and in ideological terms for the promotion of racial equality. Before we assess the organisations in more detail in terms of potential and constraints, it is important to make reference to their principal activities and organisational features.

Community relations councils are most generally known for two specific aspects of their work. One of these is their support for and advice work with racial minorities. This includes case-work over immigration, individual experiences of discrimination, welfare benefits, as well as more group-oriented advice on matters such as project funding, setting up new organisations, etc. Specific projects, such as a hostel for Afro-Caribbean youth or a day centre for elderly Asian men, are also often undertaken by CRCs. The other well known aspect of CRCs' work, is the role they play in terms of liaison with local institutions. The form this takes can vary, across the 100 CRCs in Britain, from scheduling visits to public institutions like schools, to liaising with other representative bodies such as the local authority.

The work of each CRC is carried out primarily by full-time staff, whose numbers vary in relation to size of the local communities of Afro-Caribbeans and Asians. The funding for the staff comes from the Commission for Racial Equality and the local authority, and the staff's particular job briefs, at least in part, reflect these employing agencies' views about the needs of the local racial minority communities. Nevertheless the staff are not accountable to either of these bodies but rather to the General Council of the CRC itself.

The General Council is the supreme body of the CRC, at least in principle. It consists of representatives of local organisations ranging from local churches to ethnic self-help groups and political parties, individuals with a particular interest in race-related matters and representatives from the statutory sector – particularly local councillors. It is the organisation's open constitution which permits this broad membership.

For the purpose of policy-making most General Councils elect an Executive Committee. The Executive Committee, along with sub-committees meet much more often than the General Council and are usually at the interface of local and internal affairs. Finally in many CRCs there are working groups or sub-committees of the Executive, where specific aspects of local race-related work are considered. In Wolverhampton these include, for example, housing, health and social services, civil and welfare rights, education, and youth and community; in Liverpool, sub-committees on housing, immigration, health/welfare and employment have been recently (1984) set up, complementing the more long standing education sub-committee, all brought together by a policy co-ordinating committee through which the sub-committees report to the Executive. The activities of these groups vary from collecting and collating local evidence of inequalities and active campaigning on local issues, to the setting up of local events and the formulation of policy proposals and documents.

The discussion below goes into more detail about the work and structure of the CRC, in the context of an analysis of the particular contribution of the organisation to the struggle for racial equality. In introducing this analysis it is important to point out that of the range of local organisations it is this one which has proved to offer the greatest potential. This is not to make any qualitative judgement about its success, but rather to indicate that other organisations, by comparison on a range of points, are less able (and less willing!) to promote the goals of racial equality and justice.

Although the criteria for this assessment are made explicit by our analysis, they evolved throughout the course of our work in local organisations, and were not imposed from the outset. As a result we would suggest that we have a strong basis on which to evaluate the function and role of local organisations and particularly CRCs. There are two further aspects of our evaluation that must be acknowledged. The first is a reminder that the political context is the one which was consistently a guide to our actions and decisions as researchers. This is obviously reflected in the data we obtained and that we made use of, to support our findings. Thus our criteria reflect openly the political context in which they evolved. It is also important to emphasise at this point that unlike most evaluations of organisations we were less concerned with attempting to objectively measure success of achievement than we were with assessing potential. This is not to say that there is no attempt to identify the accomplishments of the CRC or other organisations but rather to emphasise that in a political situation like the existing one, where there continues to be a saturation of inequalities and a dearth of political will to eliminate them, the factor of potentiality is enormously important.

The potential role of CRCs

The Community Relations Council is most often considered as just another local organisation concerned with responding to the needs of racial minority groups. This is because it is often the case that some of its main activities are performed by other local organisations. It is also the result of, as suggested above, the disposition of the local authority, which tends to lump 'black organisations' together, whether it be for the purpose of funding, participation or representation of demands. The effects of this attitude by the local authority is pervasive in terms of wide-spread local thinking.

In fact the CRC is distinct from other local organisations in a number of different ways. The most fundamental of these arise as a result of the origins of the CRC. In 1968 the second Race Relations Act created the Community Relations Commission and gave it the right to fund and co-ordinate local work in race relations (Section 44). As a result local CRCs were jointly funded by the Commission and the local authorities. The Act did more, however, than oblige governments to give financial assistance to local racial minority groups and their organisations. It also provided a framework within which the nature of local race relations work could be defined, for it legislated against racial discrimination and for equal opportunity. The CRCs, from 1968 then, had both security and purpose through the power of legislation.

There is a further characteristic of CRCs which is an aspect of the original organisation, and this is the nature of its membership. The committees which predated CRCs consisted of groups of people representing a range of local organisations such as the local churches, other voluntary organisations, and the local authorities. After 1968, many of these committees became the local CRCs and the principle of a broad-based multi-racial membership became an inevitable feature of the local organisation. These three original conditions, the strong funding base, the breadth of local representation and the definition of purpose supported in law, have ensured the development of the CRC. They have ensured a base from which grassroots organisations and the local race relations lobby can articulate and present their position on local race issues. They have effected an alliance of people and organisations which has the potential to exert a significant pressure locally and at a sustained level. Finally they have created a forum where the politics of race can be the struggle for racial equality rather than a nest of sectarian wrangling and self-interest.

It is rare for a local organisation taking up race-related issues to have these potential features and this is often a result of the conditions within which they arise and exist. In both Liverpool and Wolverhampton there were no other organisations which compared with the CRCs in this respect. For example, the Merseyside Anti-Racialist Alliance on the one hand was broad-based in its membership and far reaching in its overall aims and activities. It had a membership including churches, Liberals and even Conservatives as well as socialists, a range of ethnic minority groups and some trades unionists. It organised cultural events such as rock against racism concerts and multi-racial weeks, anti-racist campaigns on immigration, police, and the ultra-right, media interventions, including setting up a regular radio programme and a weekly local newspaper column and policy development work in employment, education and health. Nevertheless it lacked a significant resource base. While this did not limit the organisation in the short-term, it did mean that there were no full or part-time staff to sustain or follow-up initiatives such as the equal opportunity campaign. In the end it was this fact that led to the shift of membership of leading activists from MARA to MCRC, where resources were available, and where the campaign could gather strength.

In Wolverhampton an organisation often compared with the CRC is the Crypt, originally a Methodist youth club catering specifically for Afro-Caribbean youth, but more recently a large scale community type of organisation with an extensive staff, offering a range of services such as counselling and training and with links to the Manpower Services Commission. Over the years the Crypt has been increasingly well-resourced, receiving monies from MSC, Urban Aid and the Inner City Programme. Although the organisation's services are used by black people and there are ample black staff, the original aim of the organisation has not changed. It was set up to meet the needs of local ethnic minority groups, which were not being met by the statutory services, rather than to oppose racial discrimination and struggle for equal opportunity. This is not to say that organisations like the Crypt do not have a role to play in achieving these wider aims, and indeed they do make an indirect contribution through their very existence. Campaigning against racial inequality in a broad institutional sense rather than just by example, however, is not an explicit objective of the Crypt and hence is not incorporated into the strategy and day to day activity of the organisation.

The Crypt is also significantly different from the CRC in its membership, management and lines of accountability. It has a conventional (voluntary group) management committee, made up of a collection of white and black local notables. Since the Crypt is not an umbrella organisation its management committee cannot claim to represent a range of local race related organisations. The role of its management committee is not to ensure community representation or accountability but rather to support the work of staff of the organisation. Unlike WCCR's executive committee, which acts as intermediary body between the organisation and the wider community, the overall orientation of the management and control of the Crypt is internal and closed.

There are in both Liverpool and Wolverhampton many other examples of community based organisations which function in a similar way to the Crypt. Their main purpose is to promote self-help or complement local statutory services. For doing this they are often recognised and given financial assistance. Sometimes they can have the effect of acting as a catalyst for change as a result of their existence or efforts, but the rarity of this must be acknowledged, particularly in the light of local attitudes towards race-related issues. On the other hand, what is of concern is the fact that these organisations absorb enormous quantities of individual commitment and effort without necessarily channelling them into identifying or tackling the sources of those inequalities.

Thus, in Liverpool, one can identify the various ethnic or cultural community centres, Pakistani, Hindu, Caribbean, Sikh and Chinese; the self-help groups Charles Wootton Centre for Adult Education, Elimu Wa Nane Multi-Racial Education Project, South Liverpool Personnel Employment Agency; the Methodist Youth Centre; the Black Women's Group; the Delado Dance

Group; the Liverpool 8 Law Centre and the Access Education Project. Together these initiatives direct considerable resources towards meeting the range of community needs currently undermined or neglected by mainstream institutions, whilst on the whole making little or only ad hoc input into developing and articulating policy to transform these institutional structures and practices.

This imbalance in organisational activity, that is giving priority to responding to the manifestations of inequality rather than attacking their origins, suggests how important it is to have a broad-based movement located within a single organisation aimed at anti-racism and equal opportunity. This customary absence of an adequate resource base for specific political and policy oriented organisations or groups only compounds the problems. Under these circumstances there is little doubt that CRCs are in a stronger position than most if not all local organisations to provide a platform for mobilisation around race issues.

MCRC played a central role in the struggle which led up to and followed the appointment of Samson Bond as a principal race relations advisor (see below pp. 101–3). It was MCRC which became the umbrella organisation instrumental in the creation of the local authority's Race Relations Liaison Committee. It organised elections to this committee and serviced the Black Caucus on the Committee. In servicing the Caucus MCRC produced policy documents which provided the basis for discussion between the Caucus and officers and politicians on the Laison Committee. These included a social services report, a package of employment proposals, various education documents, the housing allocation study and a policy for racial harassment. Of particular note was the existence of an active MCRC education sub-committee which played a key role in preparing policy proposals and negotiating them with the Liaison Committee. It is in this role, as a resource to the local black community, that MCRC has been the object of community power struggles.

WCCR's campaigning and pressure group role is less developed than MCRC's partly because its resources have been concentrated on the development of its MSC training programmes, i.e. on its community development role. Nevertheless there is growing evidence which confirms the organisation's increasing involvement in the area of campaign activity. The 1980s has been an important period for WCCR in consolidating and utilising its own resources, whilst at the same time minimising its internal divisions. During this period it has submitted a number of policy reports on youth to borough council committees including the Race Relations and Equal Opportunity Committee, where it made its submission to the borough's Youth Review. WCCR's own policy committee created in 1983 has also been engaged in ongoing dialogue with the Labour Group on the council. At these meetings, WCCR has been particularly vocal in campaigning for adequate consultative machinery which would provide the means for much closer involvement of black communities in policy development. The controversy surrounding arrangements for funding posts under S11 has been at the centre of these discussions and WCCR has been instrumental in highlighting deficiencies in the development of the policy at a local level. The virtual absence of black faces on the council's side of these discussions and the minority of white faces on the other confirms the need for a more vigorous implementation of the town's equal opportunity policy. This includes the need to develop extensive and genuine forms of minority participation if Wolverhampton's black community is not to continue to remain effectively disenfranchised from the decision-making process.

Internal constraints

Within this general recognition of the scope of the CRC, we would have to concede the fact that CRCs often fail in taking advantage of their potential. This failure cannot and should not be attributed to individual personalities or any particular CRC. Rather we would say that it is primarily linked to the fact that the internal organisation and structure of the CRC is unusually complex and its membership of volunteers and staff often very large. Questions of control and responsibiity, lines of command and channels of policy formulation are often blurred; political views are sometimes diverse and conflicting and sectional interests too do not always coincide. That this is not inevitable can be best illustrated by the fact that on particular local race matters, all sections of the organisation are able to join together and demonstrate their views. Nevertheless, there is ample evidence to show that CRCs have not been as effective as they might have been in affecting local policy, and it is this that we are particularly concerned with here.

Ideological divisions Interestingly and ironically, despite the whole range of organisations and political affiliations represented on WCCR and MCRC, broad ideological differences, in terms of issues relating overtly to race, rarely surface in any consistent or predictable way.

In the case of MCRC, conflicts have been mainly over the control of the organisation as a whole, particularly between a more 'traditional' ethnic alliance with white liberal support on the one hand and a more activist grouping including the locally born black community on the other. The balance of power has tended to oscillate between the two poles over the last five years, with the struggle at times undermining the unity and credibility of the organisation as a whole. A particularly crucial issue for the two factions has been the composition of the Race Relations Liaison Committee, elected at meetings of representatives of all local black groups and race relations agencies.

In the case of WCCR the lack of ideological sharpness is in part due to a tendency within the organisation to concentrate on internal issues and conflicts related to the management of the organisation rather than on external targets in the struggle for racial equality. What differences emerge at this level do so out of conflicting ideologies of management, and, although not always, have a tendency to fall along a continuum: at one end a more democratic, participatory and permissive regime is promoted whilst at the other an emphasis on leadership and formal accountability to leadership is encouraged.

Management/staff relations Central to these differing interpretations of management is the role of full-time staff within the organisation. As we have already indicated WCCR is an extremely complex organisation, one of the largest CRCs in the country, in which a number of its potential strengths have at the same time proved weakening in terms of their effects. One such strength, at one level at least, lies in the breadth of voluntary representation, which provides a potentially rich depository of community services within the organisation. The sovereign body of WCCR, its Council, comprises this voluntary community membership which thus constitutionally at least stands in a position of superiority over the full-time staff. The latter, however, do not always perceive the organisation in these terms. According to staff, the voluntary bodies of management, Executive Committee and Council members themselves are invariably removed from the day to day running of WCCR. Many voluntary members attend only one meeting a year, the AGM, and others only attend one or two meetings a month on average. Under these circumstances it is claimed voluntary members have much less right to control working conditions and exercise judgement over external political including policy issues than staff themselves. In this sense the legitimacy of the organisation is not always fully sanctioned by the staff, a factor which may ultimately account in part for the relatively high turnover of staff membership.

The funding of local CRCs The staff's position is complicated still further by a factor which relates to the funding of local CRCs. Although WCCR is formally the staff's paymaster, it does not ultimately hold the purse strings. These are held by a number of outside bodies including the local authority, the Commission for Racial Equality and the Manpower Services Commission. Some of the arising complications can be illustrated with reference to the largest of WCCR's funding bodies, the Manpower Services Commission. In 1984 the MSC, who pays the salaries of approximately 125 (Community Programme and YTS) staff at WCCR issued a revised set of terms which WCCR were required to meet in order to be eligible for funding for the year 1984–5. One condition included the termination of funding for all cultural projects, such as arts, drama and music which, as it happens, had developed highly successful links with local schools and were at the time performing an important educational role both for WCCR staff and trainees and the institutions with whom they had established contacts. Furthermore MSC reduced the number of senior supervisors and supervisory posts and attached more specific job responsibilities to those posts which it was prepared to fund. The prospect of redundancies provoked, predictably, considerable concern within the local branch of ASTMS which held a series of discussions with senior management at WCCR. The important point to note in this respect was MSC's refusal to negotiate directly with the union, on the grounds, it is claimed, that negotiations were an internal matter for WCCR management and the union to resolve. The complexity of funding arrangements and relatedly patterns of control within the organisation thus prevented direct negotiating channels from being established. Much of the union's anger and frustration was thus vented on a management who were effectively not managing the decisions being taken. The ramifications left the organisation with a number of redundant staff, an embittered union and an impotent and unpopular management. The only body to emerge apparently unaffected was MSC who, of all parties to the dispute, was arguably, the most culpable of all.

Difficulties arising from funding are not restricted to staff. Management too has come into conflict on a number of occasions with its funding bodies. In one case at WCCR a dispute erupted over the appointment of the Senior Community Relations Officer in 1978. The conflict centred on an applicant whose application was supported by WCCR but vetoed by the funding body, in this case the CRE. In the course of the dispute, which dominated internal activities for over a year, the administration and finance of WCCR was placed in the hands of a trust body. Meanwhile, the CRE sought, without success, to wrest control from WCCR management, through the creation of an alternative rival local organisation. Ultimately however, local management capitulated to the CRE, a new SCRO was appointed, and the CRE abandoned its efforts to set up an alternative CRC (see also Ben-Tovim *et al.*, 1981a). At the most obvious level, the WCCR/CRE dispute was one about power and control, but more specifically it revolved around differences of opinion about the role of staff in CRCs. It is not surprising therefore that these and other problems should manifest themselves in the staff's experience of the organisation. The position of Senior Community Relations Officer (SCRO) is particularly indicative of this ambiguity. As senior officer he/she has clear responsibilities for the implementation of management decisions. On the other hand he is likely to be a member of the ASTMS (Association of Scientific, Technical and Managerial Staff). This dual role clearly creates dilemmas for the SCRO who is perceived both as an employer (a hirer and firer) and as a union comrade. One leading member of Wolverhampton's Asian community likened the SCRO's role to that of walking out into the middle of a battle's crossfire, on a minefield, located at the edge of a cliff with eyes blindfolded and hands tied at the back!

The above examples illustrate the potentially volatile nature of Community Relations Councils. As an organisation a CRC is in constant danger of finding itself diverted from external struggles for racial equality towards internal conflicts arising from the complex and sometimes ambiguous chains of command, including the organisation's relationships to its funding bodies, or from internal factionalism amongst key groupings.

One consequence of this tendency to become embroiled in internal management-related disputes is that the organisation fails to make full use of its membership's experience and expertise. Leading representatives from local Afro-Caribbean and Asian organisations, political parties, youth organisations and welfare groups and teachers, probation officers, and community workers are asked to make decisions about staffing and finance, and to approve and ratify reports rather than discuss issues related to local race politics and policy. The CRC thus becomes an administrative, 'political' (in the sense of committee-based) body removed, in the eyes of many of its members, from its face-to-face community, youth, welfare and advice work. It is, however, on the basis of their experience in this kind of work that many voluntary members come, or are sent, to the CRC on a representative basis.

Coordinating casework, project development and campaign activity The size and complexity of the CRCs frequently mean their various activities remain distinct and uncoordinated. The lessons of their significant casework role are not always translated into broader policy demands, and thus remain removed from the campaigning function of the organisation. Similarly project initiatives like the hostels for Afro-Caribbean and Asian women in Wolverhampton, and one for young black people in Liverpool are not always used as resources and examples from which pressure for more widespread statutory policy change can be exerted. The projects, if they succeed, remain as one-off initiatives which moreover tend to remain under CCR's umbrella rather than acting as catalysts for broader policy changes and a stimulus to further forms of community development.

In one final, perhaps most crucial respect, the organisation's impact may be limited; that is in terms of its political role, campaigning for local and national change. This role can be developed in a number of ways, not least of which is representation on, and liaison and negotiation with, local statutory bodies. WCCR for instance has access to the Race Relations and Inner Areas Committees of the borough council as well as the three police liaison committees and the Area Manpower Board in Wolverhampton. WCCR's official view of its relationship to these bodies has always been ambivalent, shifting from a position which rules out the prospect of change through participation, to one which acknowledges the opportunity of access provided by them and the need for WCCR to have a context in which to articulate its position on a range of issues within the remits of those bodies. Although it is true to say that WCCR's impact, through its solitary representative on the Inner Areas Committee, and its two person representation on the 30 strong Race Relations Committee, will always be limited, the limits of that role have by no means been tested to the full. Only one detailed policy submission has been fed into the local authority machinery through the Race Relations and Equal Opportunity Committee. Similarly no initiative has been undertaken within WCCR in terms of campaign activity as a result of knowledge acquired through representation.

WCCR's relation to the various police liaison committees in the town provide further evidence of the ambivalence in its position when it comes to deciding on appropriate contexts for the development of its campaign strategy. In the autumn of 1983, WCCR passed a policy document outlining the terms on which it was prepared to liaise with the police. As a result the organisation's representatives were withdrawn from the liaison committees. These committees, for all their defects, provided the only ongoing context within which WCCR's demands on local policing could be expressed. Thus attempts to reform the fundamental weaknesses in the committees, including their constitutional base and membership, could no longer be debated. As it transpired WCCR staff continued to sit on these committees for many months without the formal backing or knowledge of the executive committee, a fact which in itself highlights many of the problems identified here which face CRCs. WCCR's activities thus became restricted to day-to-day negotiation and consultation with police liaison staff, invariably linked to casework, and participation in a national campaign of opposition to the Police and Criminal Evidence Bill before it became law.

The ambivalence on this issue thus reflects a more fundamental ideological division within the organisations: strains of oppositionism developed alongside positive promotion and campaign activity alongside welfare oriented casework. Overall, our experience of CRCs (including a Chairperson and member of staff in Liverpool and a Vice-Chairman and Executive Committee member in Wolverhampton) convinces us of their potential significance in the development of local struggles for racial equality. They, of all local organisations, provide the basis for a breadth of representation unrivalled in our local experience and capable, through their resources, of pressing for and effecting change at a number of different levels. They struggle against a set of formidable external obstacles which seek to marginalise their impact and a range of internal constraints arising from their size, complexity and ideological breadth, which inevitably limit the realisation of their potential.

Conclusions

Throughout this chapter we have stressed the significance of local organisations in identifying and turning the issue of racial inequality into an object of political struggle. The organisations with which we have been linked have varied in respect of their objectives (which have in turn affected the particular nature of their struggle), the resources at their disposal, their internal organisation and their relationship to local power structures. Anti-racist, community and campaigning organisations all have specific roles to play within the broader struggle for racial equality. The strengths of each can be of potential benefit to the other two. Our own energies as a group have in the main been concentrated in campaigning and pressure group activities. In the long run we assess these to have the most potential in terms of challenging policies and practices on a continuous and a constructive basis. For all their problems and constraints, and we have not sought to underestimate these, CRCs and local Labour parties have provided important political contexts for those committed to work actively for racial equality. Apart from an individual's place of work, these organisations alone have provided a base from which a challenge can be made: one which, as we shall see in the next chapter, confronts the formidable forces of resistance, present at many levels within the formal political and bureaucratic structures of the local state.

5 Local Struggles for Racial Equality

The analysis of local politics and struggles for racial equality which we develop in this chapter has emerged out of our involvement in local organisations, the focus of discussion in the previous chapter. Our participation in local campaigns and our involvement in consultative and pressure group activity has brought us into contact with officers and politicians of the local authorities in both Liverpool and Wolverhampton. More specifically, our knowledge of those local political structures has developed on the basis of our involvement in equal opportunity and housing campaigns in Liverpool and political interventions in the fields of education and youth provision in Wolverhampton.

In order to make sense of and to analyse the raw data of our political experience we have worked within, and at times consciously outside, a number of traditions and positions within the social sciences. We have already identified a number of these in previous chapters. Given their significance to the central arguments contained in this book they are worth repeating, at least in summary form. They should help to locate and clarify the analysis which follows. The first concerns the relationship between research and politics. Although prevailing academic wisdom does advocate such a distinction between the two, most authors in the field of race relations do nevertheless align themselves to a particular value standpoint, for example the promotion of racial harmony, the elimination of racial discrimination or the deracialisation of labour. Despite the intrusion of value judgements in this way into race relations research, however, very little attempt is made to develop the implications of these value positions in any systematic way. In the main, political and policy recommendations, where they appear, remain somewhat hollow and gestural, devoid of political context and failing to contribute in any significant way to the realisation of these recommendations.

Our research, in contrast, has focused on concrete struggles over racial inequalities. Our direct involvement in those struggles has facilitated the production of knowledge and a process of research which takes account of local conditions and contributes to change as directly as it can, in the light of these conditions. Although this has not ruled out the possibility of producing objective research evidence, for example surveys and case studies of institutionalised racism, what we have done is to allow local conditions to dictate research priorities and to use research findings to press for institutional change. Our intervention has served to facilitate and develop our political analysis.

The tendency towards academicism (which the distinction between research and politics implies, in our view) is all the more surprising in the case of contemporary Marxist analysis, given the latter's commitment to social transformation. Instead of vindicating itself in terms of its contribution to political practice, much contemporary Marxist writing appears content to establish its fidelity to a particular interpretation of classical Marxism in order to establish the credentials of its own position. Moreover, the overall direction of much of this analysis is fostered by a misplaced reliance on Marxist economic theory at the expense of the development of an analysis along the lines of Marx's own political texts. The latter are rooted in an analysis of class forces and prospects for socialist and communist organisations as well as the (highly complex) role of the state and the implications for struggle.

Our analysis will clearly depart from these texts in terms of content and level of analysis. Nevertheless the idea of integrating theory and practice through an analysis of a highly specific and complex set of historical conditions within the context of a broadly based set of socialist objectives is consistent with the analysis undertaken in this chapter, of local struggles aimed to secure greater equality, justice and power for racial minority communities.

The study of race itself has thrown up a variety of perspectives, each developing its own analysis in terms of a particular conception of race, and the nature and source of racial inequality. In this book we have chosen to focus on the politics of racial inequality, and particularly the role played by political forces in both reinforcing and reducing those inequalities. We are not concerned, therefore, with exploring race relations in terms of culture or in terms of biological differences where those are said to manifest themselves in intelligence or (in the case of sociobiology) in innate tendencies to compete and discriminate on racial grounds. Nor do we wish to explain race relations or racialised labour in terms of class inequalities, capital accumulation and patterns of migration. This is not to suggest that race does not have a cultural or class dimension nor even a symbolic significance attached to biological 'differences' (e.g. colour). Our interest in these perspectives is with the secondary role assigned by them to the analysis of politics and political intervention. In playing this secondary role, politics comes to be regarded as a kind of residue for autonomous activity, what is left over after the principal determining factors, such as culture, biology or the economy, have exerted their influence.

In focussing on the political dimension of inequality we do not believe that we are entering some kind of autonomous sphere, where action takes over from structural constraints. On the contrary, our analysis below will establish a formidable set of limiting conditions which make political advance at best slow. What prospects there are for advance however are not assisted in our view by a knowledge of 'minority culture' *per se* without subordinating it to a discussion of minority rights and demands for institutional provision, and how such provision can be secured. Nor is the struggle for racial equality advanced by theories that racial discrimination and conflict are biologically inevitable. On the contrary, such arguments can only serve at best to legitimate political inaction and abstention and at worst to reinforce existing inequalities. Even if we were to accept that competitive and discriminatory behaviour results from genetic adaptation (which we do not), the latter must itself develop in response to environmental conditions. These conditions are by no means fixed but contingent on a complex interplay of factors including politics. Consequently the development of a political analysis which takes change as its focus could, indirectly, serve to reverse rather than merely acknowledge those genetic factors which are said to give rise to racial discrimination.

Finally we are not convinced that an analysis of racism and/or racial inequality which takes economic laws of capital accumulation, migration and declining rates of profit as its starting point can contribute very much to the struggle for racial equality. The economy does have a role in the political analysis of race, but not to the exclusion or subordination of those political processes to which it is subject. In other words the economy can be analysed as a political arena in which policies and practices with regard to investment, employment and management that serve to reinforce racial inequalities can be set against forces within the labour movement or the anti-racist movement which seek to redress them.

Our conception of politics therefore is not restricted to formal governmental institutions but refers to a mode of analysing institutional structures and relations in general. Within these institutional contexts, it focuses on sites of struggle and conflict the outcome of which cannot be predicted in advance. The contingent character of those struggles rules out the possibility of constructing a general theory of politics and/or the state. Power can no longer be conceived in terms of fixed quantities ascribed to individuals on the basis of some preconceived hierarchy of the state. Instead we need to establish those conditions which make the exercise of power possible such as law, control over policy administration, access to material resources and prevalent ideologies, and the struggles which ensue around those conditions. The development of an analysis in this way has implications for how we assess reforms and policy initiatives. These are the tangible outcomes of those struggles and however gestural they might appear they have the potential to provide the means for further advance. They serve to redefine those conditions referred to above and hence help to establish the balance of opposing forces. In this chapter therefore and throughout the book we conceive race policy initiatives not as necessarily tokenistic or correct solutions but rather as resources whose outcomes depend on the mobilisation of forces for and against racial equality.

Although there exist numerous possible contexts for undertaking the kind of political analysis developed in this chapter, our own context is necessarily limited in focus. First it is primarily local since conditions in the late 1970s and early 1980s offer considerably more scope for political interventions in this arena than at central level. Our statuses as provincially-based professionals and local activists too have shaped the focus of our analysis. Moreover those struggles in which we have been most actively involved have centred in and around local government, since this has been where local anti-racist forces have devoted much of their energies during this period. This in part can be understood in terms of the relatively greater opportunities for access and intervention provided by local government and hence the increased prospects of some limited advance.

Our analysis begins with a consideration of one overriding experience of local governments from the standpoint of local organisations. This experience can be encapsulated in the notion of marginalisation. The means by which the process of marginalisation operates is linked to those conditions referred to above which in turn provide the basis for the exercise of power. We consider examples of these conditions in the second part of the chapter. The role of anti-racist forces working to redefine the balance of forces through pressure for political, including policy reforms, will be considered in part three.

Marginalisation: experiencing the local state

We begin our analysis by attempting in general terms to capture our experience of the local state. One process which has come to reflect that experience, perhaps more than any other, is that of marginalisation. By this we refer to a prevalent tendency within local government to seek to push anti-racist forces away from the centre towards the periphery of local politics and policy provision. Local struggles against racism have thus become struggles against marginalisation. It is in this context that we have identified a number of marginalising tendencies which have remained constant throughout our political experience. Although in terms of their implications they afford little room for optimism, any degree to which the formal apparatus of the local state has been pressured into making some form of response, as we shall see, is a testimony to the significance of local struggle and a justification in itself for further intervention.

Marginalisation through consultation

Governments of all political complexions both general and local have attached, at least nominally, some significance to the involvement of local comunities in local decision-making. Race related policies and policy documents have, albeit sometimes ambiguously, laid stress on the need to consult minority communities. Consultation as a principle attracts support across the political spectrum, and has been incorporated in policy documents produced by all of the major political parties. The reality of consultation, however, in our view can hardly be said to represent a significant advance in terms of an extension of local democracy. On the contrary, and almost without exception, the variety of consultative measures in which we have been involved or have observed close at hand have served to emphasise inequalities between consultors and consulted. This has been the case irrespective of the particular form of consultative measure.

Committees, located within local government structures, have become an increasingly popular form for increasing local consultation. These sometimes have statutory status, as do the Race Relations Committees in both Wolverhampton and Liverpool. At other times they are created in response to a particular issue or crisis, have only informal links with the existing committee structure and thus take on a semi-statutory status. In each of these cases, however, elected representatives, sometimes attended by local officers, sit alongside representatives of local organisations, and overall the committee has a brief or remit, however loosely defined this may be.

Although statutory and semi-statutory committees would appear to provide the 'best' opportunity for consultative exercises to involve serious dialogue and responsible action on the part of local city councils, the experience of local organisations on Liverpool's Race Relations Liaison Committee demonstrate the circumstances of community powerlessness even at this level. Devoid of any rights or sanctions, the Black Caucus of the Race Relations Liaison Committee witnessed formal decisions regularly ignored, or directly opposed, in the Policy and Finance Committee; or in some cases in the leadership caucus of the Party Group, from which the Black Caucus is excluded. It became possible therefore, for Liverpool's Housing and Finance Chiefs to turn down (in 1984) a £1 million DoE sheltered housing scheme for the ethnic elderly, S11 funding for a team of four ethnic housing liaison officers, and a working party on racial harassment – despite the fact that they had been approved by the Race Relations Committee. The leadership's opposition to special provision thus took priority over their commitment to consultation.

Perhaps, however, the problems which dog consultative committees can best be exemplified by the actions of the Labour Group in Liverpool's Race Relations Committee over the winter of 1984/85. The crux of the affair was the appointment of Liverpool's first Principal Race Relations Adviser, a person who was to head a Race Relations Unit including six other people. Against the wishes of the Committee's Black Caucus (who, it should be noted, had been nominated to serve on the panel), the short-listing panel included for interview an applicant who had had no prior serious involvement in the area of race relations. When interviewed along with five other candidates, this person was identified by the six Labour councillors as most suitable for the job, against the advice of the union representative as well as those representatives of the Black Caucus who were also present at the interviews. These objections were based on the appointee's lack of relevant qualifications and experience, and his stance on racial inequality which he subordinated to the more general issue of urban deprivation and class inequality. It is telling that the candidate preferred by the Labour Group was later quoted as saying that he believed in

the present strategy of the Liverpool City Council . . . for the development of a systematic anti-racist policy within the framework of a broad social programme to tackle the fundamental problems of urban deprivation which, after all, are the root cause of racial disadvantage.
(Press Statement, 12/11/84, as quoted in *Black Linx*, Dec. 1984).

Representation on a statutory committee of a local authority is the closest an organisation can get, in an official capacity, to the sources of power. Yet this example shows clearly that the power of the consulted is restricted to concurring with the consultors. It also demonstrates that the consulted have no procedures for ensuring that Committee decisions are binding or that Committee actions reflect the spirit and object of the Committee. For example, the Race Relations Unit, proposed by the Black Caucus and finally accepted by the Race Relations Committee, was amongst other things to have advised the Council on how to implement its equal opportunity policy more effectively and deal with complaints of racial harassment as well as combat racism within the various departments of the local authority. The fact that the appointment of the race relations adviser was to undertake such responsibilities might justifiably have been used to question the choice of candidate, had any consultative powers existed.

A second form of consultation is to be found in the variety of one-off public meetings organised by local authorities in response to the increasing demands by community groups over the last decade. They include day conferences, seminars, workshops and exhibitions on a range of issues and are viewed by members and officers of the local authority as consultative exercises, insofar as they are concerned with community-linked issues. The fact is, however, that most often they fail to provide the opportunity for the exchange and development of ideas, let alone for the making of policy. On the contrary, they are more likely to create a false consensus, and a context in which dissension and conflict are covertly, if not openly, discouraged; and recommendations, statements of intent and even written reports which emerge from them are likely to be disregarded.

A third form of local consultation is the ad hoc meeting which involves politicians and officers on the one hand and representatives of local organisations on the other. This obviously differs from the committee in that it has no statutory status and therefore is subject not only to termination at the discretion of the elected representatives but also to their whim and will for the nature, aim and action of the meetings. Consultations in Wolverhampton with local organisations over funding arrangements under S11 provide a clear example of the problems encountered here. In March 1984 the Home Office issued a revised set of arrangements for funding which obliged local authorities to consult with ethnic minority organisations as a part of submitting their claims. Other ad hoc meetings, concerned with this issue, had taken place over the previous two years and there was some indication that it was the intention of the authority to involve WCCR at appropriate stages in drawing up the submission.

Despite this expectation, the submission to the Home Office, the first under the new arrangements, was made without any consultation. The document made no attempt to identify existing postholders, which had been the main source of grassroots discontent, nor was any attempt made beyond some very general remarks to establish detailed job descriptions or underlying strategies for the development of multi-cultural education, as it is called in Wolverhampton. Leaders of the Labour Group, under pressure from their own councillors who were concerneed about the party's prospects in the run-up to the local elections and also disturbed by rumours that letters of complaint were to be sent by black organisations direct to the Home Office, called a meeting with representatives from WCCR. The meeting which resulted highlighted many of the fundamental weaknesses of consultation. These centred around differences in power between the political and officer leadership on the one hand and WCCR on the other, and manifested themselves in such things as: control over the agenda and the direction of the discussion; control over the information that was to be made available; control over those decisions that are negotiable and those that are not and, ultimately, the power of veto. Overall the difference on that occasion, as on others, was that the Labour Group could consult who and when it chose to, while WCCR were at the mercy of Labour Group's discretion.

The failure of consultation, as a means for a more equal balance of power or more open policy making, has been documented before. Our intention, however, is not only to confirm these failures, but also to help to explain the actions which local organisations and committed activists are forced to take as a result. We shall develop this in the next section. Perhaps even more importantly, this critique should be used to suggest the components of a new framework for new political relationships. In other words, consultation may not be inevitably a failure but may instead be capable of being transformed in the context of a set of principles which operate to limit and create power.

Anti-racism as extremism

The absence of any genuine forms of participatory machinery has encouraged alternative kinds of community response to emerge. In Wolverhampton for instance, black organisations sent a letter of complaint about the authority's failure to consult. Over the same issue (that is Section 11) they threatened to boycott the local elections, and in one instance to put up an independent candidate. Such actions were dismissed as naive and extreme by local Labour politicians but were nevertheless predictable given the options open to local organisations.

Similarly, the appointment of the Principal Race Relations Adviser in Liverpool forced black groups to undertake a variety of protests, a sit-in, a disruption of a council meeting, a march and a regular vigil outside the municipal offices which were used by the Labour Group to label, isolate and undermine their opponents through slurs of 'self-appointed leaders', using 'alien' [*sic*] methods of protest, encouraging 'violent' activities and 'dividing the working class'.

It is not only the various kinds of reaction described above which attract labels of extremism and fanaticism. Equally unacceptable is the content of anti-racist arguments, which is often dismissed as hysterical, outrageous or fanatical. Anti-racist arguments are described in these ways because they fall outside local bureaucratic definitions and interpretations of race problems such as those which explain race problems in terms of cultural differences. These official definitions, articulated by principal officers and administrators, have become deeply embedded in professional policy and practice. Their respectability and apparent neutrality often serve both directly and indirectly to legitimise local popular racist opinion.

Anti-racism, since it challenges the prevailing norms inherent in institutional policy and practice, is thus inevitably regarded as extreme. This is particularly the case insofar as local organisations are encouraged to resort to direct action, protest, accusation and demonstration. In our experience there is a tendency for politicians and professionals to capitalise on the more extreme manifestations of anti-racism and to use them as a pretext for inaction rather than responding systematically, as a matter of principle, to the problems to which anti-racist activity is a response.

In Wolverhampton the 'turban case' involving Mr Noor, a leading member of the Indian Workers Association (GB), provides a good example of some of the above points. A Sikh pupil was sent home from a local school by the head-teacher for wearing a turban. In the protest following the incident, the head-teacher's actions were described by Mr Noor as racist, and the allegation was printed in the local *Express and Star*. It was these comments which provided the basis for a libel suit which was successfully filed against Mr Noor with damages of £50,000.

Mr Noor might have won this case had it been commonly accepted that actions which effectively discriminate against racial groups can quite legitimately be described as racist. The head-teacher would then, in preventing the pupil from conforming to personal religious requirements, have been guilty of indirect discrimination at the very least. The official view however was that Mr Noor had over-stepped the bounds of reason and that his allegation of racism contributed a gross aspersion on the character of a local head-teacher whose contribution to multi-cultural education was officially well regarded. Linked to this, and working against him, was Mr Noor's reputation for making 'outrageous' remarks on race issues, with the case being popularly presented as a battle between the forces of extremism and moderation.

Mr Noor's struggle, although not successful in itself, was however, part of a broader more successful struggle to put institutionalised racism on the political agenda. In common with the broad strategy pursued by anti-racist organisations he sought to bring terms like racism from the extremes or margins of political debate, into official argument. That racism has become increasingly acknowledged not only in judicial decisions but also in policy documents, committee reports and ministerial interventions must in part be attributed to community struggles like Mr Noor's.

Funding cultural initiatives

There is a tendency on the part of local authorities to restrict race relations initiatives to one-off, high profile measures rather than to develop a sustained, mainstream-oriented programme of action. This tendency is in part a reflection of trends within central government philosophy and funding policies. In particular inner city initiatives including the Urban Programme and more recently *Policy for the Inner Cities* (DoE, 1977b) have provided a framework within which funds, somewhat ambiguously, have been made available for meeting the 'needs' of minority groups. The term 'ethnic group' becomes significant in this political context since resources are thus linked to ethnic or cultural differences or needs.

Inner city policies have been directed on a selective basis to those geographical areas of highest social need including both Liverpool and Wolverhampton. Resources have thus been allocated to fund a range of local centres and projects for Afro-Caribbean, Asian and Chinese communities. In general the funding of these centres and other limited project initiatives provide confirmation that measures are being taken by the two local authorities, a fact which may be expedient in the aftermath of street conflicts or riots of the late 1970s and early 1980s. At the same time such funding can serve to divert attention away from racial inequalities which are institutionally generated and/or maintained through mainstream provision. The failure to link these ad hoc cultural initiatives to any kind of participation in formal political processes has further served to immunise local institutions from more fundamental and sustained pressure from local organisations and groups. Not only are cultural initiatives expedient, visible and non-threatening through their isolation. They are also relatively cheap, particularly for local authorities who are able to claim approximately 75 per cent of the total cost of their programmes from central government.

The discrepancies in Liverpool City Council's relationship with the Chinese community illustrates some of these points. The authority funds a Community Centre, some Centre staff, and gives high profile support to the Chinese New Year celebrations but for some time refused to support a Chinese social work unit within the social services department. Since funding under the Urban Programme and Section 11 had already been secured, it can only be assumed that the unit's proximity to areas of policy development was a major source of resistance on the part of leading Labour politicians.

Similarly the case of the Afro-Caribbean Cultural Centre in Wolverhampton confirms a number of the above points. The original decision to fund the Centre under its first Inner Areas Programme 1978–79, has been linked both inside and outside the civic centre to street conflicts involving young black people in January 1978. The authority, in the words of the Chief Executive, needed to be seen to be doing something. The Centre remains (in 1985) very much an ad hoc initiative as far as the Afro-Caribbean community is concerned. Like the funding provision for WRPA (Wolverhampton Rastafarian Progressive Association), the initiative remains relatively isolated, out on the margins of mainstream provision. Under these circumstances the Centre has found it difficult to establish itself as a significant political constituency within the town and as a base for the realisation of political objectives. In order to survive financially its priorities have remained cultural in

orientation, that is in the sense of leisure and recreation and the
use of the premises for music, drama and religious purposes.

Conditions which serve to marginalise anti-racist forces

Local political ideologies

We have suggested above that power in social relations could be
analysed in the first instance in terms of those conditions which
create the potential for its effective exercise. In this section we
shall identify a number of such conditions, the first of which has
been the prevalence of a particular form of racial ideology referred
to elsewhere as colour-blindness (Ouseley, 1982), so called
because it fails to acknowledge the specific dimension of racism
and racial inequality and consequently resists any attempt to tackle
racism independently of the patterns of urban deprivation or class
inequality. Its strength lies in its compatibility with various shades
of political opinion and its consequent accommodation within certain brands of liberalism, conservatism and socialism as well as the
universalistic ('apolitical') ideologies and practices of public
administration and practitioners. Each of these broader ideologies
in turn is able to justify action, or more strictly in the case of
colour-blindness, inaction, through a defence of the supremacy of
individual rights, national interest or class struggle over the needs,
disadvantages and rights of racially defined groups.

What binds the threads of colour-blind ideologies therefore is a
resistance to acknowledge and/or challenge racism except when it
is defined in the very narrow sense of overt and conscious discrimination. These ideologies vary on the other hand in the ways in
which they justify or explain this resistance. We refer to many
examples throughout this book but we shall illustrate at this point
some of the main forms of colour-blind ideologies insofar as we
have encountered them in the course of our political activities. The
first is based on the belief that to acknowledge racial discrimination and to highlight differences between groups is to exacerbate
racial tension and hence discrimination and make it correspondingly harder to eliminate. Liverpool's Chief Education Officer
expressed such a view in his response to the formation of the
Merseyside Anti Racialist Alliance in 1978. In it he claimed that to

allege racial discrimination is to incite discord. Similarly in their submission to the Home Affairs Committee on Racial Disadvantage, Wolverhampton Chamber of Commerce and Industry wrote 'the problems of ethnic minorities will be due as much to the Race Relations Act as any other reason' (House of Commons, Home Affairs Committee, 1981a, p. 897).

Colour-blindness can also suppress the particular experiences of black people by equating these with the experiences of other social groups. The two kinds of group most popularly cited in this respect are other ethnic groups on the one hand and the working class on the other. The Education Officer cited above remarked elsewhere that he did not believe that the system was any more rigged against blacks than against the Liverpool Irish, Welsh and Scots (*Liverpool Echo*, 29.9.78). Such views were reinforced in the *Liverpool Daily Post* some two months later where it was claimed, 'The situation in Liverpool is simply this. There is no racial problem. There are problems of unemployment, of crime, of hooliganism. They are problems which trouble both black and white alike' (*Liverpool Daily Post*, 24.11.78). Militant socialists do not hold inner city residents responsible for the city's problems, which is what might be inferred from the above editorial comment. The problem for Militant is integrally bound up with a capitalist economy and its class divisions. Nevertheless a similarity of viewpoint between the *Liverpool Daily Post* and the local Labour leadership does exist in terms of their common insistence that black and white experiences and inequalities are broadly the same and originate from the same source.

Colour-blindness can also be linked to the policy objective of integration and the principle of universalism both of which have served to discourage debate on racial inequality. In Wolverhampton, resistance to the notion of separate youth facilities on the basis of a policy of integrated youth provision is an example of this. What in fact this principle ignores is that *de facto* segregation and the effective exclusion of minority groups already exists either because of the nature of the facilities provided, or, in case of Asian girls, precisely because of the application of the principle of integrated provision. The adherence to integration had been endorsed throughout the 1970s by the then Director of Education in Wolverhampton who refused to entertain the principle of special provision. Hence a long waged struggle to combat the complex forms of institutionalised racism within education has been consistently resisted by senior education officers and a clear majority of teachers who prefer to work within a universalistic, 'treat them the same' ideology rather than with the ideas found amongst a minority of the service committed to positive change. Ad hoc consultative machinery has been used to exert pressure on senior officials to provide information, and to reform detailed aspects of policy and practice. But the sporadic nature of consultation, the resource available to the community, the continuity of professional involvement, its control over information and its capacity to pursue traditional bureaucratic traits of perceived self-interest, inertia and defensiveness can pose a formidable array of obstacles in the way of effective intervention from below.

Colour-blindness can also seek to equate examples of anti-black racism and discrimination with examples of black prejudice against white and cases of black groups, such as Afro-Caribbean, discriminating against other minority groups, such as those from the Indian Sub-Continent. This was a consistent theme of the views expressed by representatives of Wolverhampton's Chamber of Commerce to the Home Affairs Committee. Racism was acknowledged but, more importantly, it was regarded as insignificant. The following extract taken from replies to questions put by members of the committee clearly illustrates this view. In it one of the representatives refers to anti-English sentiment abroad, and of perjorative references to 'Poms', 'Limeys' and 'Sassenachs':

> I am not saying there is no prejudice and intolerance in the Wolverhampton area; I was saying it was both ways and I would not regard it as unduly significant (House of Commons Home Affairs Committee, 1981a, p. 898).

Our final example of colour-blindness is overtly concerned with the policy implications of refusing to acknowledge racism and racial inequality. More specifically it rejects positive action as a form of preferential treatment, however much existing practices are shown to favour the indigenous white population. In one case, a set of recommendations made by the CRE, which were aimed at eliminating unfair recruitment practices at Unigate Dairies, those of advertising jobs internally and informally, were condemned by a Wolverhampton Labour politician who also castigated the CRE for making them. Although common amongst Labour councillors in Liverpool, in Wolverhampton such attacks on positive action have been made, in the main, by the Conservative group on the council and generally aimed at the sort of projects for minority groups described above. Conservative politicians in Wolverhampton are assisted in this respect by the local newspaper which cultivates and strengthens links between racism in political discourse and public opinion through provocative headlining and the reconstruction of debates in terms of opposition to 'cash handouts'.

Overall therefore particular forms of socialist, liberal and conservative ideologies can each appeal to an understanding of inequality and its policy implications which effectively pre-empts an acknowledgement of the specific dimensions of racism and its implications for positive action. In doing so each appeals to forms of reason and morality which insofar as they continue to prevail serve to undermine the force and credibility of anti-racist politics. The latter has thus the formidable task of forging links with positions across the political spectrum which appear seemingly incompatible, but which converge in the common refusal to acknowledge the specific character of racism and racial inequality along with the policy implications which follow from this acknowledgement.

Our experience of the formal apparatus of the state suggests that racial inequalities, insofar as they are acknowledged, are not primarily justified in terms of genetic inferiority or a natural tendency to discriminate against minority groups. In official circles the more overt forms of racism give way to colour-blindness which we have argued is equally disabling in terms of its effects on positive action. If biologically related explanations have a role it is in their popular appeal within sections of the wider local community and as exemplified at regular intervals in the columns of the local press. Their appeal in this respect can clearly serve to underpin and to sanction official inaction and more covert forms of racism and thus make it that much harder to mount an effective challenge to racism in its local institutional forms.

Legislation and central policy initiatives

In general, central policy initiatives on race add up to a patchy, somewhat inconsistent framework comprising laws, policy statements, directives, circulars, reports, regulations and consultative machinery. Insofar as race has become an issue centrally, it has been confined to a number of special policies which have served to reinforce overtly negative perceptions of the race problem for example policies on immigration and policing. Secondly it has also provided an extremely loose, permissive and ambiguous framework within which positive policies need or need not be developed locally. Examples of this approach are the Urban Programme or the Race Relations Act with their non-directive support for positive action initiatives. Finally the 'special' nature of these initiatives has left a whole range of policy fields untouched in terms of providing directives, regulations and terms of enforcement for the development of positive initiatives at a local level. Consequently the ambiguous, ambivalent character of central initiatives can be used both in support of and in other circumstances in opposition to political ideologies, like colour-blindness, operating at a local level.

Section 11 of the 1966 Local Government Act exemplifies all three of the above characteristics and, although we shall examine it more closely in the next chapter, a number of points can be made in the context of the arguments being developed here. Section 11 was not in terms of its inception a measure designed to redress racial injustices or promote racial equality. It was more a form of financial compensation paid by central government to certain local authorities for staffing expenses arising from the settlement of immigrants and their associated 'problems' within their local areas (Young and Connelly, 1981). In this sense then Section 11 serves to reinforce negative views of black people and to legitimise local hostility to their presence. The absence of any positive framework for the specific allocation of the monies available allowed local authorities to claim funding for staff salaries without developing special job responsibilities or even, for the most part, identifying Section 11 post holders.

In Wolverhampton (Liverpool were not able to claim funding until 1983) successive controlling groups on the council failed to use Section 11 to develop positive policies although clearly this option was open to them given the basis of the original provision and the absence of any attempt by central government to monitor local spending patterns. Indeed, in Wolverhampton the local Labour group have defended their failure to make positive use of Section 11 on the grounds that central government had not required them to do so. Even local organisations themselves only took up the issue with the change in arrangements governing funding of Section 11 in 1983. Their aim was clearly to turn what had long been a generally negative measure in to one which had some positive pay-off in terms of redressing racial equality. Finally, it must be said that even if Section 11 had been used positively it would nevertheless have always remained a 'special measure' and its central administrative location within the Home Office would have prevented it from providing a means for a fundamental rethinking of mainstream policy within local education authorities, social services and other departments.

Financial constraints inhibiting redistribution

Cutbacks in central government's financial support to local authorities, alongside increased controls on how local government allocates its resources, can provide strong additional arguments for resisting positive change. What is perhaps more revealing is the consistency with which positive action has been resisted over the past twenty years irrespective of changes in the levels and form of financial control by central and local government. In our view economic austerity and growing central control over local budgeting are not as significant in themselves as they are in terms of the pretexts they have provided for further inaction.

In our experience many proposals emanating from local organisations and aimed at eliminating institutional racism have at best entailed no additional cost and at worst required the redistribution of current expenditure. The expansion of the black workforce within the local public sector; the attachment of equal opportunity conditions to contracts with the private sector; the creation of participatory structures within local government involving black organisations and parents in the running of public services; the expansion of a youth counselling service at the expense of traditional youth club provision and the allocation of black applicants to council properties on an equal basis to whites, are all possible within both the limits imposed by central government and local pressure to minimise rate increases. In our experience attempts to resist these and other proposals on grounds of cost reflect a more deep-rooted unwillingness to acknowledge inequalities and the need for positive action.

In conclusion to this section we would argue that there exist strong forces within local government which can and have, in our experience, militated against the use of the local public sector as an instrument of positive social change in the pursuit of racial equality. Deep seated cultural traditions within the town hall foster political styles of rhetoric and posturing amongst politicians which serve to alienate the vast majority of apolitical constituents and to demoralise those actively committed to positive social change. These party political traditions offer little in the way of a challenge to local authority bureaucracies which are thus left to themselves to exercise considerable control. This control is exercised both defensively and self-interestedly and invariably justified in the name of administrative neutrality. What is perhaps most disturbing of all, in our experience, is the extent to which both politicians and officers have joined forces in the face of pressure from anti-racist forces from outside the town hall. In the course of their active conscious collusion which we have witnessed directly in the context of consultation, they have employed with considerable sophistication what may be regarded as somewhat clichéd but nevertheless prevalent practices of gerrymandering and filibustering in order to withstand the pressure from representatives of the community.

Forms of anti-racist struggle

The marginalisation of anti-racist forces and the conditions which make marginalisation possible have been the focus of the first part of the analysis undertaken in this chapter. The purpose so far has been to establish the context in which racism is challenged and racial equality pursued. In what remains of this chapter we examine three different forms of struggle, each of which offers its own particular challenge to racial inequalities.

The three forms of struggle, spontaneous protest, pressure for community resources and planned political struggle, reflect a variety of responses to the problem of racial inequality. Although all three are committed to challenging racism, some are more explicit and specific than others in defining their objectives. Strategies vary accordingly, since each form of struggle has its own priorities and its own understanding of how best these might be achieved (cf. Ben-Tovim *et al.*, 1982b).

The effects or consequences of struggle may be quite concrete, such as a positive redistribution of resources, or more abstract and less tangible such as an acknowledgement of the role of institutionalised forms of racism in creating and maintaining racial inequality. These reforms, which result from struggle, help to re-define the conditions of future struggle and hence should in our view play an integral role in the development of anti-racist strategy. The significance which we attach to calculation of this kind is responsible for the emphasis we place on planned political struggle. Overall our assessment of change *vis-à-vis* racial inequal-ity, which we take to be the focus of our analysis, is thus based on, and will vary according to, those conditions analysed in the previ-ous section and the particular forms of anti-racist struggle which we discuss below.

'Riots' as an issue in local politics

Spontaneous street protests are significant not only because they have proved important catalysts for reform, but also for the way in which they have become issues in local politics. Contrary to much press reporting and some political interpretations, the 1981 disturb-ances were probably not part of an orchestrated strategy on the part of those involved. Nor can they be dismissed as hooliganism or criminality and hence non-political. In our view spontaneous protest has through history and up to now represented a significant form of political intervention, which although distinct from other forms to be considered below nevertheless remains a legitimate object of political analysis.

Our concern is not so much with disentangling the causes of the 1981 conflicts but rather with identifying the *effects* of the riots, particularly in terms of policy-making and mainstream political practice at a local level. Our experience here reveals that whatever the insurrectionary nature of street conflict, its major impact, iron-ically, probably, for many of its advocates and participants, can only be described as reformist. In many respects disturbances or the threat of them have been a more effective lever and instrument in local reform, notably in resource allocation, than have those political forces for whom such change constitutes an integral part of their political practice.

Wolverhampton had already witnessed street conflicts in its

recent history prior to 1981. In 1979, disturbances outside the George public house precipitated a local community enquiry into allegations of both police harassment and police indifference/ inaction in cases of racial attack. The most visible effect of those disturbances, according to at least one officer of the council (Interview, Environment and Technical Services Department, Wolverhampton, October 1978), was Wolverhampton's designation as an Inner Area Programme Authority. And as a result of this the Local Authority supported the funding of an Afro-Caribbean Cultural Centre amid considerable local protest. The disturbances in July 1981 provoked a similar official response in this respect. They were used to justify funding for the local Wolverhampton Rastafarian Progressive Association, and the Liverpool 8 Law Centre in Liverpool.

Local Afro-Caribbean, Asian and anti-racist organisations have been more concerned to use street conflicts as an opportunity to articulate their ongoing concern over local policing policies and practices, the problematic aspects of which are highlighted during periods of local unrest. Such was the response to the 1979 disturbances in Wolverhampton when local organisations compiled a dossier of racial attacks, many of which it was claimed had been met with indifference and hostility by the police. At a one day conference on 'Police and Black Youth' held at WCCR in May 1982, local organisations and community leaders confirmed allegations of police harassment of young blacks in the courts following the street conflicts of July 1981. Not surprisingly, West Midlands Police Committee proposals for extending consultative machinery were met with considerable scepticism by many of the participants at the 1982 conference. The basis for such proposals appeared not so much to develop forms of community participation in local policing, but rather to secure more efficient policing under the guise of consultation. This scepticism seemed all the more justified in the light of a police proposal for lay visiting whereby individuals were to be allowed to enter police stations on the understanding that community leaders and others would intervene to placate sections of their respective communities in the event of further disturbances. The funding of youth projects under the auspices of the Crypt organisation as well as the employment of leaders from the Crypt as mediators, in the event of local disturbances and conflicts, has been interpreted by many as part of an attempt to strengthen the control element of local policing in more subtle and covert ways and hence serve to enhance the legitimacy and support for existing policing practice.

The form of response on the part of local statutory bodies to periodic street conflicts or the threat of them has however remained consistently ad hoc and gestural. That responses are invariably made in the *wake* of these 'crises' and not as a matter of principle or, for that matter, in response to formal and informal pressure through conventional political channels must encourage a cynical view of local policy development (cf. Edwards and Batley, 1978). Whether these 'panic' responses take the form of one-off projects, or impromptu meetings of national or local politicians with community leaders, they are rarely followed up. Furthermore, such responses have consistently belied an absence of political will on the part of statutory agencies to tackle in any kind of sustained way the problems of racism and racial disadvantage.

Pressure for community resources

Community and project work, which incorporates explicit commitment to racial equality, varies considerably in the range of its activities. Supplementary schools, projects for young offenders, and the provision of welfare rights counselling are examples of the various forms it can take. Across this broad spectrum of activities, community and project work seeks to meet the perceived needs of the community through the making of provision which either supplements or represents an alternative to mainstream provision. In principle this kind of activity brings organisations into direct daily contact with members of the community who seek help on an individual basis or through group activity. Hence casework and project development have become important features of community work organisations.

The pursuit of these objectives has brought some organisations into conflict with local authorities. In Wolverhampton two organisations concerned with youth related activities, Wolverhampton Rastafarian Progressive Association and the Crypt, offer an interesting comparison in this respect. WRPA have struggled for premises and resources against a background of media hostility and, at least initially, local authority resistance. Eventually as a result of direct action including a sit-in protest, mass lobbying and sustained pressure, the group were provided with premises in a disused school.

In contrast to this form of pressure which has emanated mainly from within the black community, the Crypt, by far the largest local community organisation in terms of staffing and resources, has a predominantly white leadership. The organisation embraces a range of youth facilities including counselling and training schemes funded through MSC and a youth club. Its success has relied much less on direct action than a combination of formal negotiation and informal bargaining. The organisation's capacity to secure resources has little to do with its successful and effective utilisation of resources. How it spends its money and on what basis, are not matters for local community scrutiny, at least not necessarily, since access to the organisation is restricted, and management and administration are the responsibility of paid staff rather than a voluntary and accountable membership. Its ability to attract funds in our view has more to do with ideologies shared by both the Crypt leadership and its funding bodies, in this case shared perceptions of 'race' problems and how best to tackle them. Applications for grant aid and informal negotiations are thus both conducted within a climate of mutual understanding and consent. Consequently there is little need to have recourse to tactics of direct protest of the kind employed by organisations like WRPA. One final point of comparison in the case of the two local organisations referred to above is worth noting. Whatever the limits of community organisations, funding in the case of WRPA does at least mean that a section of Wolverhampton's young black community is in a position to define its own needs and to have direct control over what limited resources are made available. This is an important principle in the case of community organisations and one which differs from that operating within a predominantly white-led organisation like the Crypt. In such cases the needs of local black communities are defined on their behalf and the (considerably greater) resources distributed accordingly.

Overall it must be said that the outcome of any community work initiative, black or white, will appear piecemeal and minimal given the potency and prevalence of racial inequality. The establishment of a supplementary school may benefit its own pupils but will not necessarily affect the vast majority of black children in mainstream education. Welfare rights counselling may benefit a minority of individual claimants in contrast to a change in policy and/or the law which may affect claimants as a whole. The significance of community work organisations therefore lies in their identification of community needs and their highlighting of deficiencies in mainstream provision. Unless these are pursued, however, in the context of struggles for institutional change then their impact will be correspondingly limited. Insofar as institutional deficiencies are tackled in this broader context, community work activity gives way to planned political struggle.

Planned political struggle: challenging local policy and the policy-making framework

A third form of anti-racist struggle can be identified as planned political struggle. It is distinct in terms of two characteristics: it is premised on a critical analysis of local/central policy and it is specifically directed at changing that policy and the policy-making framework that underpins it through the development of sets of strategic demands.

As well as entailing a different approach to racial equality from that of spontaneous protest and community based work, planned political struggle effects a different type of response. Whereas 'riots' produce arbitrary sets of reforms and community-based work supplements existing provision, planned political struggle represents a series of challenges to those conditions which serve to marginalise anti-racist political forces. Throughout this chapter we have stressed the contingency of those conditions, that is to say that their realisation or otherwise depends on the outcome of political struggle which in turn depends on the nature and characteristics of anti-racist forces. Furthermore the effect of these challenges varies, and successes often turn out to be momentary and gestural, with what appear to be advances turning into retreats.

Although the organisations we have supported have been involved in campaign activity we would not for the most part describe their involvement in this way. Campaign activity in our experience stands for organised political struggle around a series of specific, finite and agreed upon objectives. Liverpool City Council's decision to introduce an equal opportunity policy in 1981 for instance resulted directly from one such grass roots campaign. In the main, however, most political involvement is less tangible, less co-ordinated and more uneven and sporadic.

Below are identified some features of the political activities with which we have been associated, each of which seeks to redress racial inequality by challenging those conditions which serve to reinforce it.

Redefining the problem A major undertaking of this kind of campaigning organisation has been to argue the case for positive action, supported by evidence of institutionalised racism and resulting inequalities (see Prashar, 1984). We have already noted the strength of colour-blind ideologies in local politics and the ways in which they act as a strong force of resistance to positive programmes for racial equality. Anti-racist forces have thus sought to provide evidence of inequalities on the one hand and in our case the compatibility of positive action with the broader political objectives of socialism on the other.

In Liverpool the production of a profile of opportunities in the city included evidence of the disproportionately low number of black workers employed by the city council (Ben-Tovim *et al.*, 1980, 1983), whilst a survey of council housing proved the dis-crepancies in the quality and location of housing allocated to black tenants (CRE, 1984b). Similarly, in Wolverhampton the inadequacy of youth facilities for groups of young people of Afro-Caribbean and Asian descent, cases of alleged police harassment, evidence of disproportionate numbers of expulsions from school and the dis-proportionately low numbers of black school governors are just some from a flow of evidence of racism and inequality (for example see WCCR, 1984).

At the heart of these debates is the question of who or what is responsible for the inequalities. The argument underlying positive action places that responsibility unequivocally on the institution. The absence of black people from employment in the town hall, Asian girls from youth facilities in Wolverhampton, black people from desirable council property in Liverpool or Asian languages from schools in Wolverhampton must be considered in terms of institutional failure to redefine job responsibilities, to develop appropriate criteria for selection, to devise recruitment procedures which ensure greater proportions of black employees, and to develop provision which is attractive to young Asian women. Redefining the problem thus entails challenging those assumptions which attribute the above problems to the lack of qualified applicants, cultural conflict within the Asian community, community housing preferences or the failure of black people to integrate or assimilate into western culture.

The implications of relocating the problem in these terms points unambiguously towards some kind of positive action, which may have been argued for in consultative meetings, in the local press, in Labour party meetings, and in ad hoc deputations to civic leaders and others. The ever present danger is that a concession to positive action might belie a cynical lack of commitment to act on its implications. Moreover, politicians and officers by nature of their political position and their control over administration are able to ignore sporadic pressure from consultative procedures and other similarly tenuous forms of community liaison.

Building alliances Those engaged in political struggle have sought in varying degrees to embrace as wide a spectrum of concerned groups and organisations from within the community in order to pre-empt attempts to dismiss anti-racism as unrepresentative of community demands (Ohri *et al.*, 1982; Ouseley, 1984). In Liverpool the equal opportunity campaign included a broad range of community representation co-ordinated through the Merseyside Community Relations Council. It facilitated a variety of forms of pressure to be exerted at different points and in a united manner within the apparatus of local government (Ben-Tovim *et al.*, 1981b, 1982a).

Nevertheless, our organisational experience has repeatedly confirmed to us the fragility of alliances. They invariably rely on a base of active support which is in reality quite narrow, however representative the views of the community spokespeople. The breadth of organisational support is often the result of a core of individuals working simultaneously in a number of organisations. The departure or withdrawal of a key individual therefore, can often threaten the survival of a seemingly broad based alliance. Collaboration between organisations, if it succeeds at all, may only do so for the lifetime of a particular issue. Invariably struggles crystallise around a set of concrete demands which in the unlikely event of their acceptance, can lead to the disbanding of the alliance structure. Even when political demands are conceded, the fragility of alliances, the lack of community resources and the skilful manoeuvring and delaying on the part of politicans and officials alike all combine to weaken the prospects for policy implementation through sustained community pressure.

Breaking down resistance   A priority in anti-racist struggle is the identification of crucial points of potential institutional resistance and the attempt to neutralise if not win them over. The significance of gaining trade union support for the principle of an equal opportunity policy in Liverpool became clear at the campaign's earliest stages. Trade unions not only represented one source of official opposition which had to be negotiated. They were perhaps more significantly regarded as crucial in terms of its implementation. The campaign therefore undertook various activities to persuade Liverpool Trades Council and later local trades unions to join the call for an equal opportunity policy within the authority.

It has to be said that the support of the Trades Council was not easily won. Campaign members who sat on the Trades Council began by actively seeking to reconvene its Race Relations Sub-Committee. It was this group who organised the survey of black workers within Liverpool City Council referred to above. The Sub-Committee met with opposition from both Militants who regarded the issue as a diversion from class struggle and Communist party members who, although more sympathetic, were also concerned that record keeping in employment would strengthen management's position in its personnel function, and that records could be used to black people's disadvantage. Separate discussions were thus held with Labour and Communist members to explain the findings of the employment survey and to convey the support of local black organisations for the principle of monitoring as a necessary instrument of equal opportunity policy. In addition to these meetings a motion supporting positive action on race was passed by the Trades Council with many black members supporting the need for an equal opportunity policy including a monitoring mechanism.

The support of local trade unions in the case of the Liverpool campaign ultimately proved crucial in the campaign's success given the marked tendency on the part of local government to respect the views of local trade unions insofar as the latter appear resistant to the principle of positive action. In Liverpool's case, trade union support thus effectively challenged institutional recalcitrance, a condition which was only realised through the development of links between trade unions, anti-racist and other community organisations.

Using central initiatives in support of anti-racist struggles The relative ease with which local authorities have been able to resist pressure for positive action is in part made possible through the failure of central government to take a strong and effective lead on racism and racial equality. On the contrary local authorities have invariably used central policies for legitimising inaction. Overall the onus remains heavily on local organisations to maximise the scope and use of central policy initiatives. From the standpoint of local organisations, central government appears removed and remote from local struggle. It rarely provides sustained and co-ordinated support, and in many situations works as much against, as for, local struggle.

For example during the equal opportunity campaign in Liverpool the CRE made a general promotional visit to the city in order to gain local council support for a positive policy in line with the 1976 Race Relations Act. Unfortunately poor organisation on the part of the CRE on this occasion including a lack of co-ordination with the local CRC seemed to do little to alter local official attitudes. Similarly, in Wolverhampton local organisations planned to take advantage of a visitation from the Home Office to press the case against the local authority's misuse of S11 funds, but effective stage management on the part of the authority as well as selective listening and adept manoeuvring on the part of the Home Office team served to silence would-be opposition.

Our overriding experience of central initiatives should not however lead us to ignore the way in which local struggles have effectively appealed to and utilised the centre both in specific instances and in a more general sense. In Liverpool, campaign activists made use of the 1976 Race Relations Act and Section 71 in particular through its general exhortations to local authorities to promote equal opportunity. Similarly in Wolverhampton, Home Office revisions to the administrative guidelines governing S11 funding were used to encourage the local authority to provide more information and involve communities in submissions for funding. We shall return to these points in more detail in the next chapter.

Lobbying local politicians and officials   Because political struggles against racism invariably take place at the margins of local government, the struggles often never reach the formal agenda of local decision-making machinery. Insofar as they do, a successful outcome clearly depends on support for specific demands by local politicians and officers. In the case of Liverpool's equal opportunity campaign much lobbying and canvassing was carried out, in the build up to the committee meeting at which the issue was ultimately debated and accepted. It had been imperative prior to this meeting that the matter was not lost in the bureaucracy, a feature of administrative control referred to above, or that councillors should debate a race related issue without adequate briefing. Hence each councillor was sent a copy of the equal opportunity submission at an early stage, rather than simply letting it appear in council papers at the last minute. Furthermore it was important, in a situation where no one political party had a majority, that delegations were sent to meet the leaders of all three parties, Labour, Liberal and Conservative. Caucus meetings of the parties were also lobbied, as were individual councillors. Here the contacts were built up between councillors, trades unionists and minority group representatives. This was accomplished through direct membership links with the Labour and Liberal Parties, common involvement in the MCRC or MARA, co-operative experience in the Ethnic Minorities Liaison Committee and the researchers' knowledge of local political and bureaucratic procedures. All of these contacts were thus used to ensure that a co-ordinated campaign was developed. Discussions were also held with several key officials, particularly the Chief Executive, who seemed to have accepted, during the course of the period with which we are concerned, that the time had at last come, to claim the collaboration with minority groups which had brought the issue to the attention of the council. The substantial black presence at the meeting confirmed the significance of the issue and clearly exerted additional pressure on councillors to support the proposal.

The achievement of all party support for the resolution is worthy of particular note in a city known more for the bitter and often mindless hostilities between all parties than for its political co-operation, a reputation for which it has earnt the local nickname 'Toytown'. It is also significant that none of the three parties represented on the city council had a single black councillor, nor indeed any substantial ordinary membership from local black and ethnic minority communities.

Having been addressed by the Chairman of the Merseyside Community Relations Council, itself an unusual mark of legitimacy for a formal Council meeting, there was unanimous adoption of the resolution which had been put forward in response to the submission of the black groups and agencies:

(i) this Committee agrees to adopt an Equal Opportunities Policy and instructs the Chief Executive to bring forward an Equal Opportunity Statement for consideration by this Committee;

(ii) this Committee supports the establishment of a Liaison Committee comprising representatives of the black community and nine representatives of this Council (three members from each political party) to be appointed at the next meeting of the City Council with the following terms of reference:

    (a) to consider what are the obstacles to the achievement of greater racial harmony in Liverpool;

    (b) to examine the way in which the City Council's policies might be extended or altered so as to contribute further towards overcoming these obstacles;

    (c) to suggest priorities in any development policy arising from such examinations; and

    (d) to report from time-to-time with recommendations to the Policy and Finance Committee, the Merseyside Community Relations Council and other bodies as appropriate;

(iii) the Liaison Committee consider, at its first meeting, the other suggestions put forward by the community groups.

(Liverpool City Council, Minutes of Policy and
Finance Committee, 9 December 1980)

The statement shown in the box was drawn up shortly afterwards by agreement between the City Council officers and the Merseyside CRC, and again unanimously accepted by the Council.

Liverpool City Council – Race Relations
Equal Opportunity Statement

This City Council declares itself to be an Equal Opportunity Council and is determined that both in its provision of services and as an employer, it will ensure equality of opportunity for all persons regardless of race, colour, ethnic, or national origins.

As regards the provisions of services such as education, housing and social services this means that the Council will take active steps to ensure that all requests for and recipients of any service are treated equally. Policies and procedures will be designed not to discriminate either intentionally or unintentionally against any group or individual. The council will also seek to respond to any special needs experienced by particular groups.

As regards employment this principle will apply to the recruitment, training, pay, conditions of employment, work allocation and promotion of staff in all parts and every level of the Authority. The Council will also make use of the provisions of the 1976 Race Relations Act which allows for initiatives to encourage under-represented groups to apply for posts, and for specific training facilities if members of an ethnic group appear to be unfairly concentrated in any one level.

It will also seek to apply these principles to all work undertaken for the Authority by external employers.

The Authority will ensure the implementation of this policy by monitoring the situation from time to time in consultation with the Council's Race Relations Liaison Committee and appropriate trade unions.

The City Council will promote, as envisaged in Section 71 of the Race Relations Act, good race relations between all persons of different racial groups within the City and will adopt policies that actively seek to encourage this.

(Liverpool City Council, Minutes of Race Relations
Liaison Committee: February 1981)

The eventual adoption by the City Council of an equal opportunity policy statement was, then, the culmination of nearly two years sustained and co-ordinated campaigning by an alliance of local organisations. This resulted in a complete about-turn in the way politicians and officials had traditionally regarded issues of race in the city. But, as the Home Office was quick to acknowledge, this grassroots achievement in Liverpool was unique. Elsewhere in our experience continuity of effort is often broken down by institutional forces of resistance. Conditions which make for the marginalisation of anti-racist forces realise themselves despite pressure from below. Even in Liverpool the successful conclusion to the campaign must be set against subsequent events. In other words even a policy decision of the significance of that of equal opportunity can only ever be regarded as a stage in a process of struggle which is ongoing and against which there can be setbacks. In the case of Liverpool, the Labour leadership has since fought and won back its control over the appointment of the Principal Race Relations Adviser. There has also been, as we discuss elsewhere, the subsequent suspension of the Race Relations Liaison Committee which was set up to oversee the equal opportunity policy.

Conclusions

Our analysis of political struggles for racial equality in local government has confirmed the integral role of organisations and of policies in those struggles, roles frequently overlooked in social science literature especially Marxist literature. Political struggle, in our experience, is marked by movements of advance and retreat which are invariably slow, sometimes imperceptible but never predictable. Of course we can say the forces of resistance to racial equality within local government can be formidable, particularly the prevalence of racial ideologies. The most common of these in our experience is characterised by a refusal to acknowledge racism and relatedly to pursue any of the steps necessary to redress it. The continuing prevalence of colour-blind ideologies within local government is made possible through the realisation of other conditions: the ambiguity and permissiveness of central policy initiatives, the control exercised at the local officer level over information as well as policy implementation and administration, and the compatibility of colour-blindness with a broad range of mainstream political ideologies.

We have argued that the above conditions are not fixed. Their realisation depends in part on the strength of the challenge from anti-racist forces, who have challenged institutional resistance through spontaneous protest, bidding for resources and planned political struggle. The last of these, of which we have most direct experience, has sought to challenge those conditions referred to above in the most specific and direct ways. That is to say it has engaged in struggle over conflicting definitions of the problem, it has attempted to pre-empt charges of extremism through the building of alliances, to break down resistance through negotiation and representation and to turn central resources from negative obstacles into positive initiatives in support of anti-racist struggles.

Reforms and policy initiatives which result in part from these struggles over conditions, help define future conditions of struggle. For this reason alone planned struggle cannot afford to ignore or dismiss reforms, such as equal opportunity policies, specialist race staff, new committees and units, and monitoring, as divisive or gestural, but to acknowledge them as an integral part of the conditions of struggle. To argue this is not to deny the fragility of advances secured through struggle nor is it to under-estimate the attack on a reform's potential through the reassertion of those forces of resistance described above. The weaknesses of anti-racist forces cannot, regrettably, be ignored in this analysis. They invariably operate within a narrow conception of what is regarded as politically legitimate, so that the task facing local organisations in their struggle against marginalisation, pseudo-forms of consultation and charges of extremism is indeed immense.

In this situation, research has an indispensable role to play in helping to politicise the issue of racism by documenting and publicising forms of inequality, unravelling the structures and processes which shape them, developing strategies for intervention and change, and linking this research to the ongoing process of political struggle by anti-racist organisations.

6 Central Policy Initiatives and the Local Politics of Race

We have considered the local politics of race primarily in terms of struggles over the issue of racial inequality; of institutional resistance to and organisational pressure for positive change. The significance of this local context, however, is mediated by wider policy contexts, especially those laid down by central bodies such as governments, committees, national organisations and company boards. Local institutional racism and any countermeasures are thus in part sanctioned overtly, or by default, by central policies and processes.

There exists a range of different kinds of central initiatives in the field of race examples of which include laws and government policy documents and circulars such as the 1971 Immigration Act, the 1981 British Nationality Act; the Police and Criminal Evidence Act (1984); the Race Relations Act 1976; Section 11 (Local Government Act, 1966); and the Inner Urban Areas Act 1978. Other initiatives include committee reports, for example, the Rampton and Swann Reports (on education); the Scarman Report (on the Brixton disorders) and the Thompson Report (on the youth service) as well as the initiatives of national organisations such as the Commission for Racial Equality, (CRE) and the National Union of Teachers (NUT). The CRE has produced documents including its Code of Practice on employment and reports on youth, social services and housing while the NUT has provided guidelines for professional approaches to underachievement, use of Section 11 and combating racialism in school. We would include all of these within our loose framework of central initiatives.

We shall consider some though not all of these initiatives and interventions in terms of two levels of political response and reaction; at the level of local government and at the level of voluntary community and anti-racist organisations. As far as local government is concerned, central policy initiatives vary widely in the extent and forms of their control. Some policies are administered regionally by non-elected officials, for example in the case of social security. Others provide greater scope for public access at a local level, for example in the case of education. In the economy, laws relating to taxation, to companies and to health and safety, and policies on investment and industrial relations for example, provide a framework within which the public and private sectors operate. The degree of local control over employment conditions depends on the specific nature of the relationship between public and private enterprises operating locally and on more central forms of control, including policy frameworks laid down by central governments. Community and anti-racist organisations by virtue of the variety of possible local situations and sometimes as a result of a more direct relationship between themselves and the centre, through their parent organisation or the relevant Whitehall department, add a further dimension to be taken account of in analysing central/local relations.

Local government and its responses to central initiatives on race

In the main our contact with local government has been the result of our participation in various forms of consultative initiatives established by both local councils in Liverpool and Wolverhampton. We have therefore witnessed at first hand the ways in which a variety of central government policies have been interpreted and implemented by both local authority officers and politicians. We have supplemented this evidence with reports, circulars, and other documents produced by both central and local governments.

Initially it had been our intention to carry out a series of interviews with officials from the Home Office, Department of the Environment and the Department of Education and Science on various aspects of government policy. These were to have been followed up by surveys of local authority officers in both geographical areas. Although we completed our interviews with

Whitehall officials, we were denied formal access to both town halls with the result that our active involvement in a number of local organisations proved our principal means of contact with both local authorities. In retrospect we believe that these forms of contact have provided us with a more reliable and accurate knowledge of the views and practices of local administrators and politicians. Responses to survey questions on race relations, as the interviews we carried out with Whitehall officials revealed only too clearly, are invariably couched in terms of bureaucratic procedures and broad but extremely vague sets of policy principles. Furthermore, opportunities to 'test' these official pronouncements against conditions and practices is limited without ongoing contact. In any event our aim was not merely to record reported views but to seek to influence policy development as members of local political and community organisations with both a commitment to their objectives and, albeit limited, resources to harness this commitment. To have operated under the guise of objective research would have been misleading, at least in the sense that we did not rule out the use of our research for policy change. To have admitted the 'political' character of our research, that is to state our concern with policy change, would have made access to local officers even less likely. Our political commitment could thus only be accommodated, and access achieved, through our already well established participation in politics. The various forms of contact which have been made possible as a result, have provided us with an opportunity to debate issues and press for change over an extended period of time. Local authority practices have thus been tested not only against present intentions but past promises, thus providing not only a more realistic appraisal of local policies and practices but a more purposeful one in terms of political commitment.

Our organisational activity has involved us in different kinds of consultative or participatory exercise, three of which have been of particular significance. The first of these is the committee mechanism which includes for example the Ethnic Minorities' Liaison Committee in Liverpool, the youth policy branch committee (of the local authority) in Wolverhampton, and an on-going consultative committee between Wolverhampton's Labour Group and the local Community Relations Council. Training courses have provided a second opportunity for contact with local officers and politicians in the housing field in Liverpool and the youth service in Wol-

verhampton. Finally, we have attended a succession of conferences, meetings and seminars on a variety of race related policy
areas. As a result of these forms of contact with the two local
authorities, we have built up a picture of the different kinds of
local authority response to central initatives. In what follows we
identify and discuss these responses mofe fully.

The use of central policy initiatives to supplement local expenditure
programmes rather than providing catalysts for mainstream policy
changes

Two 'early' policy initiatives aimed at providing additional funding
at the local level were Section 11 of the 1966 Local Government
Act, and the Urban Programme followed by Policy for the Inner
Cities (DoE, 1977b). In the case of Section 11 the initiative had its
origins in the Labour Party's commitment in the 1964 general
election to some form of special aid for 'immigrant areas'. This
commitment was spelt out in the White Paper *Immigration from*
the Commonwealth (Home Office, 1965). In it the Government
combined its support for immigration control with a support for
policies designed to enhance the integration of immigrants.

This intention to integrate immigrants should not be regarded as
recognition of the problems of racism and racial inequalities. On
the contrary both central and local government were more concerned with those disadvantages inflicted on the host community
than with those experienced by the immigrant groups. Furthermore, the problems of inner city areas, such as overcrowded
schools and the lack of public sector housing, were popularly attributed to the presence of the immigrant groups themselves.

Throughout the 1960s local authorities made it known that they
held central government to be responsible for the numbers of
black immigrants in Great Britain and subsequently for not taking
any action to prepare local areas for their presence. In response,
central government introduced a clause (Section 11) into its Local
Government Act 1966. This clause permitted monies to be made
available to local authorities where the presence of New Commonwealth immigrants caused them to require additional staff to
deliver their services. Clearly it was government's hope that this
grant aid would distract local authorities, and the wider public,

from the more controversial race issues. On the other hand, it is equally clear that Section 11 was not an attempt to either attack racial disadvantage or secure equal opportunity in employment for racial minority groups.

There is evidence of this in Circular No. 15/1967, the Home Office's first guidelines for local authorities. Alongside the procedural details, the circular identified the 'type of staff' who could be considered as satisfying the criteria of 'work attributable to differences of language or customs': liaison officers, interpreters, 'teachers appointed specially to deal with the language or other problems of Commonwealth Immigrant children', additional payments to heads, deputy heads and perapatetic teachers; school anciliaries, educational welfare officers, social workers. This list is indicative of the Home Office's intention that Section 11 be used for the development of English as a second language, and to bolster the numbers and salaries of staff whose work brought them into face-to-face contact with the most recently arrived Asian and Caribbean immigrants. Further evidence suggests that 80 per cent to 90 per cent of Section 11 monies have been used in this way by local authorities. In 1980, the DES submitted a memorandum to the Race Relations and Immigration Sub-Committee of the House of Commons Home Affairs Committee in which, in Para. 14, it says: 'In 1978–9, grant under Section 11 was paid on local authority expenditure on education totalling about £33 million, mostly for providing specialist teachers of English or of remedial skills' (House of Commons, 1981a).

Although there was never any intention for Section 11 to affect the employment levels of racial minority groups, it was assumed that Section 11 would benefit black people as a result of the increased numbers of specialist workers. As Section 11 has increasingly become the focus of local concern, so it has come to light that many LEAs have not even used the grant aid specifically in relation to racial minority groups. On the contrary the monies have often been used as a means of improving inner city schools' teacher/pupil ratios. Many local authorities eligible to claim under the terms of Section 11 appear to have done so in the main to supplement their mainstream education budgets. The grant has not therefore been used to rectify deficiencies in institutional provision and the inequalities to which they gave rise. This local interpretation of Section 11 is well illustrated by Wolverhampton's then Director of Education who wrote in 1977 in response to the EEC directive on mother-tongue teaching:

> We don't count the numbers and have had no census since the DES saw fit not to count ethnic minorities. I am concerned not just about the cost but because this is not the way to get an integrated society. We would resist any move in the direction of specialist provision for any particular culture. That is a slippery slope and it would never stop.
> (Cited in *Education*, 8 July 1977, p. 20.)

Wolverhampton, it should be noted, was at the time the local authority with the highest grant-aid per 'New Commonwealth immigrant' under Section 11!

Like Section 11, the Urban Programme/Inner Cities policy provides extra cash to local authorities on an area priority basis. The priority given to geographical areas rather than specific groups has meant that the framework within which the policy has been developed has always had a certain ambiguity or inexplicitness with respect to the importance of race within the total project.

In terms of its origins there seems little doubt that the Urban Programme was introduced in 1968 against a background of popular concern and debate on race relations (see Edwards and Batley, 1978). Indeed, the programme was announced only days after Enoch Powell made his famous 'rivers of blood' predictions. Similarly, the Inner City Policy initiative in 1977 was supported in the House of Commons by Peter Walker, who made explicit reference to the lessons to be learnt from inner city violence in the US in the previous decade. Despite these links between race and inner city policy, both the Urban Programme and the Inner City White Paper and the political pronouncements surrounding them remained peculiarly ambivalent over the relationship between race problems and inner city problems and their solution.

With respect to the Urban Programme, the then Home Secretary James Callaghan insisted that the Programme was designed to alleviate 'those areas of special social need' including but not exclusively aimed at those areas with a relatively high immigrant or black population. Indeed the Programme was introduced in such haste that no clear objectives or strategy developed. There was no clear classification of what constituted social need, and no clear criteria were established for the selection of areas and projects. The Urban Programme has been widely criticised for its piecemeal ad hoc programme and its relatively limited impact with respect to meeting racial minority needs. Only one phase of its stages of implementation, phase 12, was devoted exclusively to black self-help projects; and it has been estimated that only 10 per cent of the programme's resources were channelled into race-related initiatives.

In the case of the 1977 White Paper the extent to which the new policy was intended to relate to the particular needs of racial minorities remained ambiguous. The initiative was considered radical by some, particularly its architects, not because of its stance on race but because it shifted attention away from the problematic characteristics of particular individuals, families or groups towards wider structural features of economic decline, physical decay and social disadvantage which are seen as key elements of the problem of the inner cities.

On the specific issue of race the White Paper adopted two quite distinct lines of argument. On the one hand it argued that the particular needs of 'ethnic minorities' should be 'fully taken into account in the planning and implementation of policies for the inner areas in the allocation of resources under the Urban Programme' (para. 19) and that minority groups in the inner areas 'need to be given a full opportunity to play their part in the task of regeneration' (para 20). On the other hand, the White Paper also argued that 'the attack on the specific problem of racial discrimination and the resultant disadvantages must be primarily through the new (1976) anti-discrimination legislation and the work of the Commission for Racial Equality' (para 19). Similarly, Peter Shore in debating the initiative in the House of Commons claimed that his purpose was to 'deal, regardless of whether there are black or white populations, with aggregated problems of poverty and deprivation in our major urban centres' (Hansard, 6 April 1977, p. 1236).

This ambivalence has been reinforced at a local level both in terms of the eligibility criteria for funding and the subsequent allocation of resources to local groups and projects. In the case of the first of these there were two major groups of local authorities that became eligible for heightened support in the post–1977

Urban Programme. Seven authorities were granted 'Partnership' status. This involved relatively large cash injections and a close link-up between central and local government, including county, district and health authorities, in the form of a joint decision-making Partnership Committee advised by officers and steering groups and normally with a co-ordinating team. In contrast the Programme authorities received a smaller cash injection and had no new local machinery to formulate and administer their programmes.

The criteria that were used to weight the various possible indicators of need, such as unemployment, derelict land, population loss, low incomes, overcrowding, proportion of ethnic minorities, were never made clear. Nevertheless, Liverpool was assigned Partnership status probably because it was one of the three cities involved in the Inner Area Studies and hence widely recognised for its levels of multiple deprivation, and also for its historical association with race riots and disturbances. The decision to make Wolverhampton a Programme authority was made partly, at least according to local officials, on the basis of the town's historical association with the race issue (largely through Enoch Powell) and in the shorter term arose out of local race disturbances which broke out in the February of the year it was awarded Programme status.

Although the presence of black populations in both Liverpool and Wolverhampton may have added considerable weight to their respective authorities' claims for additional resources, the black people themselves have received a very low proportion of the available funding. Although financial support for race-related projects across the country has climbed from £8 million in 1981/2 to £12 million in 1983/4, it remains only a fraction of the total budget of £215 million in 1981/2 and £348 million in 1983/4 (Department of Environment, 1983, pp. 1, 4). In the case of Wolverhampton, the Minister with responsibility for race relations in the Department of the Environment wrote to the Local Authority in 1984 complaining of the lack of support being provided for race-related projects (some 3 per cent of the total budget). The lion's share of the resources was being used to fund economic and environmental projects. In neither type of project was the possibility of accommodating a positive race relations dimension acknowledged.

Both Section 11 and Inner City policy initiatives have provided an opportunity for the development of positive local policies on race which in the main has not been taken. Although central government, as we shall argue later, has not gone out of its way to direct local authorities to use central resources in a positive way, neither has it prevented them from doing so. Instead, what resources have been made available have been used to bolster up expenditure programmes, under pressure from both central government cut-backs in rate support, and from local ratepayers intent on minimising their liability for the cost of local public services.

The suppression of central policy initiatives in the interests of administrative expedience

There is a second way in which the scope if not the spirit of central initiatives has been subverted at a local level. It relates to a process at work in local authorities which 'depoliticises' initiatives for the sake of administrative convenience and, in so doing, sacrifices the potential scope for a positive response at a local level.

In the case of Section 11, prior to its revision in 1982, this depoliticising process was facilitated by a framework imposed by central government. Within that framework there was no machinery to ensure that local councillors and officials were aware of the existence of Section 11. The National Union of Teachers was thus able to report that in one authority (in 1978) the Chief Executive did not know about Section 11, and in another that it was only as a result of the NUT survey itself that the authority decided to apply for grant-aid (NUT, 1978b, p. 15). Our own research in Wolverhampton in 1979 indicated widespread ignorance amongst officers and councillors of the fact that the authority was obtaining grant-aid under Section 11. This situation can be partly explained by the passive nature of government circulars on Section 11, the first of which (No. 15/67 in 1967) was addressed to the Town Clerk with one additional enclosed copy for the 'Chief Financial Officer'. Decisions as to whether and to what extent local authorities applied for grant aid were obviously left to the discretion of at most a handful of principal officers.

The style of the Home Office was equally non-interventionist in cases where local authorities *did* submit claims. In the first place it offered no advice or guidance with respect to how Section 11 monies could be used by local departments, and sometimes it appeared almost to try to discourage innovatory use of a grant. At an interview at the Home Office in 1979 with a civil servant who had responsibility for Section 11, we were told of a spate of recent enquiries about the appropriateness of Section 11 for setting up steel bands in schools. It is ironic that although the Home Office did not know details of how big spenders of Section 11 were using staff, they nevertheless demonstrated concern as to whether teachers of steel bands were justified under Section 11 as the result of 'difference of language or custom'.

Up until the early to mid-80s, however, it was more usual for local authorities to submit substantial claims for block grants on the basis of calculations made by finance officers and personnel of individual 'user' departments, such as education and social services. There is evidence from our own investigations to suggest that at least until 1979 in Wolverhampton, this was a common occurence. Detailed information about the roles and deployment of staff was not specified in the claim, nor was it demanded by the Home Office. Had this been the case, the Home Office would have monitored all claims. There was, however, no monitoring function linked to the implementation of Section 11, and apart from anything else, this meant that the Home Office could not ensure that Section 11 monies were being used in accordance with the principles enshrined in the law.

The failure of the Home Office to actively advise on and monitor the use of Section 11 encouraged local authorities to adopt the same approach. Instead of Section 11 providing the basis for a positive policy response to local racial minority groups, the local authority were thus able to subvert its potential and turn it into an administrative device for bolstering up mainstream revenue.

An attempt was made by the then Labour Government in 1978 to revise Section 11 in the light of growing criticisms from both within government and beyond (Home Office, 1978b). The Bill, however, fell with Labour's defeat in 1979. Further criticisms of S11 followed however, and these were highlighted in the Rampton report on educational underachievement (Committee of Inquiry, 1981, pp. 68–9) the Scarman (1981) report on the Brixton disorders (section 6.34) and the House of Commons, Home Affairs Committee (1981a). The Conservative Government ultimately responded with its own revised guidelines contained in two Home Office circulars (97/82 and 94/83).

The new administrative arrangements had some effect of widening the scope and impact of Section 11. Abolishing the '10-year and two per cent rules' effectively meant that some British born black communities qualified for a local authority to make a claim. The new arrangements extended the eligibility to include an obligation on the local authority to provide detailed information about new posts, and also to consult with local CRCs or the local 'Commonwealth immigrant community'. Finally the arrangements also proposed the regular review of all existing Section 11 posts.

Although the revised guidelines have increased the geographical areas and the types of posts funded (along the lines proposed in the unsuccessful Local Government Grants (Ethnic Groups) Bill, and in such a way as to undermine criticisms of the most overt abuses of the fund), they have still not developed the means by which the Home Office can ensure that local authorities make a coherent response, and undertake meaningful consultation or effective evaluation. Suggestions, such as the guidelines make, that these are significant aspects of policy implementation are no substitute for machinery which is set up to carry out these tasks. Although the revised guidelines have increased the geographical areas and the types of posts funded, they have not introduced mechanisms by which the Home Office can ensure a coherent response, meaningful consultation or effective evaluation on the part of local authorities. The absence of these mechanisms in fact was identified by 'consumer' groups (e.g. the NUT, CRCs) as the most significant problem with Section 11 at the time of the Home Office's consultations (see *Hansard*, 29 March 1979, cols 280–82). Local officers and politicians throughout the country, however, were less concerned about these institutional procedures and more vociferous about the eligibility issues. It is therefore probably not surprising that the new arrangements broadened the basis for eligibility.

Similarly, in the case of inner city policy, local authorities have capitalised on central government's ambivalence on the issue of race. Beyond one or two one-off initiatives, local authorities have made little attempt to develop policy structures which deal explicitly with racial inequalities in the inner cities. In both Liverpool and Wolverhampton, levels of black participation in the planning and implementation of the policies and in the 'regeneration' of the inner cities (DoE, 1977b, paras 19 and 20) have been low, despite central guidelines to the contrary. In Liverpool, there was a brief period of optimism, when it was thought that participation might be developed beyond ad hoc contact with individual agencies or the odd public meeting, or discussions with voluntary agencies to consider priorities for funding. However, the establishment of the forum which provided the basis of this optimism, a Race Relations Sub-Group within the Social and Environmental Working Group of the partnership structure, dissolved after a few inconclusive meetings. Its failure reflected the lack of a clear brief for the Sub-Group, a passive approach by the central agencies and a negative attitude from most of the local officers who were content to take no action and to wait for the CRC to produce some detailed proposals.

In Wolverhampton participatory and consultative processes have involved a combination of public meetings, representation of the WCCR on the Inner Areas Sub-Committee and annually the circulation of *draft* copies of Inner Areas Programmes to the Race Relations Committee and voluntary agencies including WCCR. None of these however, have provided a basis for participation in the sense of involving organisations and groups actively in the development and implementation of the programme.

The failure to develop effective forms of participatory machinery reflects a failure to break with what seem to be standard administrative practices in local government. In Wolverhampton, decisions regarding the identification of key districts in the town earmarked for additional support, the weighting of the distribution of monies between economic, environmental and social projects and finally decisions regarding the support or continuing support for voluntary projects, are all by and large made by officers and brought to the Inner Areas Sub-Committee for approval.

The absence of any formal criteria, apart from the general stipulations made every year by central government, for selecting projects for funding severely limits any kind of comeback on officers either from the Inner Area Sub-Committee itself or from agencies outside the local authority structure. The small percentage of the budget allocated to racial minority projects is, in the first instance, due to the absence of minority representation where it counts, that is to say in the departmental structures of the authority. The lion's

Loan Receipt
Liverpool John Moores University
Library and Student Support

Borrower ID: 21111056405111

Loan Date: 29/03/2010

Loan Time: 5:20 pm

Race and health in contemporary Britain /
31111007660861

Due Date: 19/04/2010 23:59

Cultural diversity in health and illness /
31111009763788

Due Date: 19/04/2010 23:59

Please keep your receipt
in case of dispute

share of the budget is thus taken up in economic and environmental schemes, neither of which acknowledge scope for the development of a race dimension. Furthermore, the budget for social projects is allocated to individual departments, and these determine their own priorities on the basis of applications received from the community which fall within their remit of responsibility. Since racial minority groups tend to apply for one of two kinds of project in particular (education and social services) their access to the social budget as a whole is effectively restricted. Finally it should be remembered that the inner city policy initiative of 1977 was acclaimed as a breakthrough in terms of its understanding of the problems of the inner city. It had, it was suggested, shifted responsibility from individuals and groups to the economic and environmental structures of the inner city. Ironically, the only race-related initiatives to emerge from the policy have not come from its new found emphasis on the economy and environment but from the remnant philosophy of the old urban programme, with its emphasis on 'problem' groups or group pathology.

The use of central initiatives to make high profile if somewhat gestural concessions to positive action

Inner city policy It has already been suggested that racial conflict or the threat of it has proved significant in the emergence and development of inner city policy from the 1960s. The level at which race 'problems' have been acknowledged, that is to say in terms of overt racial conflict, has in turn helped to shape central government's response, through highly publicised cash handouts to the inner cities. These cash injections appear large in absolute terms but are relatively small by comparison with other forms of central support for local authorities and certainly disproportionate to the amount of public attention they receive. By the same token, local authorities have responded in ways which complement and reinforce the highly charged and sensitive context in which a number of initiatives have been introduced. This has been further encouraged in Wolverhampton's case by the circumstances in which it became a Programme authority in the wake of local street conflicts between young blacks and police.

Local authority interpretations of the inner city initiatives have then in turn focused on one or two high profile initiatives thus continuing a pattern of funding carried over from the old Urban Programme. Consequently in Wolverhampton the only concession to race in the first of the programmes in 1978 was the funding of the Afro-Caribbean Cultural Centre, which by the Chief Executive's own admission (in an informal discussion) was an attempt to be seen publicly to be doing something. Similarly in Liverpool, funding was made available for a Chinese Cultural Centre in the first year of the Partnership programme, thus adding to Pakistani, Caribbean and Hindu centres funded under the earlier Urban Programme. Other race-related projects, scattered across the range of local authority provision, have also been funded. In Wolverhampton, support has been provided for several training workshops, the Crypt Youth Centre, a centre for the Wolverhampton Rastafarian Progressive Association and Sikh Temple. In Liverpool various self-help groups have been supported including staffing for South Liverpool Personnel employment agency; Elimu Wa Nane, Charles Wootton and the Access education projects; the CRC's homeless youth hostel, and its Asian Worker and Public Education Officer; the authority's black home help scheme and a contribution to the Liverpool Law Centre.

In some respects it has been easier to justify funding cultural centres, projects, etc. in Wolverhampton than in Liverpool. The 'problems' arising from a relatively new (i.e. post-war) population of immigrants has been more readily interpreted in terms of cultural differences and diversity. In so doing it becomes possible at the same time to sidestep the issues of racism and racial inequality. In contrast it has been harder to interpret the 'problems' of Liverpool's long standing black population in cultural terms. In its efforts to avoid acknowledging racism. Liverpool City Council has often prefered to equate race problems with the region's economic decline and hence to subsume the solution under some broad economic initiative. This means that the high profile, albeit gestural response of funding one-off cultural projects is less evident in Liverpool. The Task Force initiative on Merseyside is a case in point. Although it was created in 1981 in the wake of the Toxteth disturbances, few of the projects subsequently funded under the initiative have any relevance to the black community. The most notable of these were a small sports centre, an information technology centre and a housing management trainee scheme.

Race relations legislation   The creation and expansion of race relations committees, units and equal opportunity policies within local authorities should be understood in part in terms of the context provided by the 1976 Race Relations Act, in particular Sections 71 and 37. Section 71 of the Race Relations Act refers to local authorities' general statutory duty 'to make appropriate arrangements to ensure that they promote equal opportunities and eliminate discrimination in respect of their functions'. This portion of the Act has been widely criticised for its vagueness and the lack of sanctions, but nonetheless it has helped to put pressure on local authorities to respond. A growing number of local councils have adopted some form of equal opportunity policy since 1976, as indeed have some other public bodies such as regional and district health authorities and the BBC as well as some private employers.

Section 37 of the Act makes it legal for private and public bodies to compensate for racial group inequalities such as disproportionate numbers of black teachers or black managers. Thus special schemes may be organised, in fields of education and training, to specifically enable black people to 'catch up' with respect to occupational levels, skills or professions in which they are under-represented. A degree of 'positive discrimination' in favour of black candidates for specific categories of employment may also be allowed within this section.

Once again, these provisions have been criticised for their *permissive* rather than mandatory nature. Initiatives have once again been left almost entirely to the discretionary mercies of local authorities, apart from promotional activities of the CRE and the diffusion of models of good practice from the more innovatory authorities themselves. This discretion has had the predictable consequence of under-utilisation of these possibilities within the Act and of enormous variations and disparities in local policy and practice between authorities, and even between departments within the same authority.

Within this loose and non-directive framework, confusion and controversy over differences between 'positive discrimination' and 'reverse discrimination' have been exacerbated, as emerged in the debate following the Scarman report. Lord Scarman himself contributed to the ambiguities here by his apparent retraction of his call for 'positive discrimination' and even 'reverse discrimination' in favour of the milder types of 'positive action' already allowed under the Race Relations Act. Thus, although the Act provides legitimacy both for equal opportunity policies and for positive action initiatives to be developed at the local level, it also provides plenty of room for manoeuvre within which critics from both the left and right can inhibit substantial use of these powers.

Despite variations in strength, scope and effectiveness of local authority equal opportunity initiatives, our experiences in Liverpool and Wolverhampton confirm their potentially fragile, superficial and somewhat hollow form.

The declaration of equal opportunity policies and the establishment of a race relations/ethnic minorities committee structure in both places suggest a nominal commitment to racial equality. The peripheral role both committees play in the structure of their respective authorities, their lack of control in terms of implementing and monitoring changes in employment practices, the lack of effective influence in mainstream spending departments, and their own lack of spending power have all contributed to their marginal role. In the case of Wolverhampton, despite the relative failure of the Race Relations Committee to make any significant impact, its responsibilities were broadened in 1984 to include women and the disabled. Representatives from Afro-Caribbean and Asian communities were asked to nominate representatives to sit on subcommittees for the disabled and women and to contribute to the production of detailed policy documents in those areas for discussion in the main committee. Moreover, there is an ever present danger that the existence of the committee can be used as a forum for gestural forms of consultation and a pretext for inaction elsewhere in the authority.

The tendency to encourage individual rather that collective responses to policy issues

Central government policies in education, social services, social security, housing, the police and immigration all provide frameworks which are redefined, interpreted and implemented at a regional or local level. One important aspect of these frameworks and their regional and/or local interpretation is the relationship between individuals and the particular service in question. In the main social services, housing etc. have all developed structures and practices which facilitate and foster relationships with members of the community *as individuals* rather than as groups of constituencies. The casework philosophy on which much social work practice is built is one example of this process. Local housing systems too are managed, with the exception of tenants' associations, on an individual/family casework basis.

One effect of this structure is the development of grievance machinery which can only accommodate complaints on an individual basis rather than on the basis of any group response. Consequently the atomisation of the service/community relationship effectively serves to undermine collective attempts to participate in and exercise control over public institutions and facilities. The position of the officer/administrator, which is already strong because he/she is able to rely on historical precedent and tradition and the knowledge of his/her system, is thereby strengthened. Professionals thus at best support individuals rather than groups of black people, in the contexts of systems, moreover, which characteristically control more than they liberate.

The process of individualisation combined with administrative control militate against the acknowledgement of group inequalities and the processes which give rise to them. Race relations committees, structures etc. conflict in this respect with the dominant philosophies and procedures which characterise mainstream provision. In the field of public housing, for instance, members of minority groups who encounter harassment on their estates, indifference from housing offices, delays in their applications for transfer, offers of accommodation on the least desirable estates with the worst amenities are dealt with by the system and confront the system as individuals. Yet those inequalities are experienced by individuals because they are members of a minority constituency. As a result the inequalities and the processes which give rise to them require a radical departure from individualised caseload philosophy and practice.

Race as a party issue in local politics

The tendencies identified so far have, in the main, inhibited rather than facilitated positive local race programmes, although as we shall see they have not prevented the utilisation of available resources by local community organisations and groups. We have argued consistently that all major political parties have remained resistant in varying degrees to positive action on race issues. Those initiatives which have emerged locally, at least in Wolverhampton, and to a lesser extent in Liverpool, have come from local Labour parties although this is not the case nationally. Local Conservative parties have been known for example in Bradford, to promote positive initiatives and even in Liverpool individual Liberals and Conservatives on the council show as much commitment to anti-racism in the broad sense of the term, as their Labour party opponents. In our experiences there are conflicting ideological tendencies in all three parties which make for degrees of ambivalence on race issues. One of these tendencies, which we might refer to as inter-party rivalry, can turn race into an issue which is pursued for the sake of maintaining ideological divisions between the parties, rather than out of any unbending loyalty to party principles.

In Wolverhampton for instance the Conservative group have opposed the funding of the local Community Relations Council, the establishment of a race relations committee, the funding of the Rastafarian centre and the Afro-Caribbean Cultural Centre. This attitude has been adopted despite the pressure from and effects of central policy initiatives such as the need for resources or the need for the authority to be seen to be doing something on race; and regardless of the fact that where Conservatives are *in control*, as in neighbouring Dudley, their position is not dissimilar to Labour-controlled authorities.

Further evidence of this ideological posturing is witnessed in the absence of any commitment beyond those initiatives on the part of the Labour Group, except in the cases of individual, and often isolated, members. It is almost as if a number of the initiatives have been conceded to grudgingly and maintained in order to spite political opponents rather than out of any underlying commitment to the principles of positive action.

Central initiatives on race: the local community response

In 1984, the Home Office in the person of its principal race relations Minister, David Waddington, made a rare and brief appearance in Wolverhampton. The purpose of the visit was not altogether clear, but opportunities were provided for local organisations and groups to raise issues of concern to their members with him. Although in one sense it was not difficult to come up with a very long list of complaints and grievances to put to the Minister, it was quite difficult for members of community organisations to prepare for the visit. Not only was the timetable of meetings and visits during the day extremely full, but more significantly this was, for many, their one and only experience of access to a government minister. It thus prompted members and staff of WCCR to consider the ways in which central government made its mark on local race relations.

Local organisations, like WCCR, relate to central policy in two ways. On the one hand they seek to make the most of a relatively weak set of central resources, such as laws, funding and reports, which can nevertheless be used to press for positive changes at local level. On the other hand, they seek to contain, limit and oppose the worst excesses of government policies which directly and indirectly provoke and maintain racial inequalities. WCCR thus prepared for the meeting on this basis although as it turned out the Home Office were evidently unimpressed by local arguments put forward. Subsequent press reports confirmed the Minister's belief that race relations had improved since the Conservative electoral success in 1979 and moreover that this optimism, it was suggested, had been conveyed to the Home Office in the course of a number of meetings with community leaders, groups, etc. around the country (*Guardian*, 6 July 1984).

In what follows we shall examine in some detail central initiatives insofar as they have impinged on two areas of local struggle in Wolverhampton: in the fields of youth and educational provision. In each case we shall look at the various kinds of central initiatives, whether these have taken the form of laws, government white papers, committee recommendations, reports of national organisations as *resources*. That is to say we shall examine them insofar as they have been used both to assist and to inhibit local struggles for racial equality. It should be stressed that the two areas selected below are by no means exhaustive of local responses to central initiatives on race, nor are they comprehensive in terms of our own political experience. We do not discuss our extended involvement in equal opportunity and housing campaigns in Liverpool. Nor do we consider here local opposition to immigration policies which has centred around the activities of anti-racist organisations in both Liverpool and Wolverhampton. To some extent these political experiences are analysed in varying degrees in other contexts in the course of the book. Furthermore our intention here as elsewhere is not to provide an exhaustive history but more an indicative and illustrative one which provides a framework for our political analysis.

Youth provision in Wolverhampton

In 1977, Wolverhampton Council for Community Relations in conjunction with the newly established Commission for Racial Equality published a report entitled, *Youth Provision in Wolverhampton*. The results of a survey of young people which formed the basis of the report, indicated that traditional youth club provision was inadequate in meeting the needs of young people. It also revealed an absence of young black people in the management of local youth services, and a failure to provide counselling services and support black self-help initiatives. The report concluded that these factors together contributed to inequalities of access and provision between black and white young people. What was needed was a broader based youth service in which traditional youth club recreational provision could be extended in order to meet the changing needs of young people and linked to other local authority departments with an interest in youth provision such as social services and housing. Since the report's publication in 1977, various groups and organisations have campaigned for a coordinated policy on youth in the town and the upgrading of the local youth service from its Cinderella status within the education department.

The joint WCCR/CRE report, in common with more recent central initiatives, have effectively provided resources which have been used directly and indirectly to legitimate pressure for reform. We have stressed throughout this book that pressure for positive action on race has invariably come from organisations and groups at the margins of local politics. Neither WCCR nor the local community workers group, both actively involved in recent campaign initiatives, enjoy much status locally. Relatively deprived of resources and access, charged with extremism, these groups rarely command the respectability and credibility enjoyed by those working *within* local government, the council officers and the politicians.

The opportunity to appeal to 'higher authorities' is a significant one in the struggle for credibility and the recapturing of the middle ground in political debate. In the course of the campaign initiatives on youth, a variety of central initiatives, including the above mentioned CRE publication, performed this important legitimising role.

Reports of national bodies   There have been two nationally based reports which have provided yardsticks as well as levers in local policy campaigns. One of these, *Youth in a Multi-Racial Society: The Urgent Need for New Policies (The Fire Next Time)* (CRE 1980), is particularly significant because it acknowledges black youth as a target group for public provision.

> The majority of young blacks live in our Inner Cities, sharing with their white peers many problems of 'multiple deprivation'. In addition, they have many problems specific to themselves, related to the discrimination and prejudice they encounter and to other disadvantages which they experience. The problems confronting youth are amongst the most crucial in the Inner Cities debate. They are issues which the Commission believe must be given highest priority consideration by Government and local authorities. (CRE, 1980, pp. 7–8)

Secondly it made explicit, where these problems originated, as the following passage indicates:

> It is sometimes easy for those in authority to regard young people as 'the problem' To do so is to confuse cause and effect. The real 'problem' lies in the inadequacies of society and the inabilities to respond to the needs and challenges of new generations of young people especially those with different ethnic backgrounds, colour and/or culture (ibid, p. 10).

The report's acknowledgement of youth as a constituency with political rights, has implications for public policy. It demands a consideration of a much wider range of public provision. Youth policy, it asserts, is not just about youth club facilities, about somewhere to go in the evening, but about policies on housing, policing, social services and employment. The emphasis is therefore away from providing an essentially leisure/recreational service to meeting responsibilities across a broad range of policy areas in order to secure the rights of young people.

Thirdly, the report made a detailed set of recommendations aimed at a radical restructuring of youth provision. Amongst these recommendations was one which proposed that local authorities establish their own youth policy committees which would be responsible for the coordination of youth provision across departmental boundaries.

The second national report resulted from a committee set up in 1981, by the then Secretary of State for Education, Mark Carlisle, to report on statutory and voluntary youth provision, both in terms of the use of existing resources and the need for legislation (DES, 1982). Like the CRE report, that of the Thompson Committee challenged age-old traditions and orthodoxies within the administration of the youth service which had encouraged a sense of complacency and inertia. The report complained of the fragmented and uneven nature of youth service provision and of the failure to involve young people in the planning of its services. It also acknowledged the potential significance of the youth service in the struggle against racism. This anti-racist role could be developed in three ways, the report argued: 'by making itself fully multi-cultural in its outlook and curriculum; by exploiting its capacity to lobby and campaign for equal opportunities and appropriate community development; and by introducing a measure of "positive action" into its management practices' (DES, 1982, para 6.38, p. 60). A continuing thrust of the report is the emphasis placed on community needs insofar as these are defined by the various sections of the community themselves. Thus the report argues: 'it should not necessarily be assumed that the youth club as such is the best instrument for meeting an ethnic community's needs ... (nor should it) necessarily be a matter of concern if the de facto membership at any particular time turns out to be all black or all white' (pp. 61–2). Some, although not all, of these arguments were reflected in the recommendations of the Thompson Committee. At a local level the report proposed that local education departments have responsibility for coordinating youth policy across the authority and within the voluntary sector. Furthermore, the participation of young people in the running of local youth services would be secured through the establishment of local youth councils.

Arguably, neither the CRE nor the Thompson reports went far enough in their acknowledgement of racial inequalities or in specifying the various forms which racism takes in the structuring and administration of policies which affect young people. The CRE report for example, has been criticised for discussing youth problems in terms of young people themselves rather than in institutional provision and practice (Centre for Contemporary Cultural Studies, 1982). Similarly the Thompson report makes virtually no reference to race in its recommendations.

Despite these flaws and omissions, both reports were invoked on a selective basis and provided important substantiating evidence in local struggles for changes in youth provision in Wolverhampton. The CRE report was cited by individuals and community organisations who sat on a branch committee of the local authority's education committee during 1981. It was made reference to, once again, in WCCR's written submission to the local youth review in 1984. So too was the Thompson report whose proposed revisions to the existing philosophy of the youth service provided an important basis for WCCR's submission (WCCR, 1984). On the positive side then both national reports helped to sanction local pressure for change. They did undoubtedly serve to strengthen the somewhat precarious position of community organisations in their struggles with the local political establishment. What both reports lacked however, was legal backing, explicit guidelines for implementing change at the local level and political pressure to do so from central government. In the case of the Thompson report, the Secretary of State after due consideration of its findings announced publicly that the Government had no intention of acting on its recommendations. What little legislation on the youth service exists, thus dates back forty years to the 1944 Education Act. We shall return to this point in the context of a more general assessment of the impact of central initiatives below.

National organisations   Both the National Youth Bureau and the National Association of Youth Clubs have provided support for local campaign activity, although it must be said, of a somewhat ad hoc and ephemeral nature. In the case of the National Youth Bureau, its information centre in Leicester provided important resources for WCCR in the development of its campaign role. Its detailed bibliography on *Young and Black in Britain* (National Youth Bureau, 1981) provided access to some of the already well rehearsed criticisms of youth service provision, some case study examples of initiatives taken in other parts of the country, and some ideas for future change.

The national Association of Youth Clubs acts as a potential coordinating body for youth clubs across the country. Like the NYB its national status provides it with an insight into national policy making. One of its members sat on the Thompson Committee Review Group. In playing an umbrella role it also has a knowledge of problems encountered and initiatives undertaken across a wide range of local authorities. The Association representative's presence at a one day conference sponsored by WCCR on youth provision in Wolverhampton in 1980 lent respectability to the demands of the local campaign. Its national status, and expertise in youth issues, added a unique contribution and dimension to the political debate on the day.

In the case of both organisations however, contact with local pressure groups was short-lived. Neither organisation played a role either before or since their fleeting involvement in the local campaign. The absence of any well-established channels of communication and, to some extent the lack of coordination, has weakened the potential role of these national bodies in supporting local campaign activity. Neither the national bodies nor the local organisations have developed traditions for making use of each other's resources on an ongoing and sustained basis. The onus thus invariably falls once again on those least equipped in terms of resources, the local voluntary organisations and groups, to maintain contact with would-be allies at a national level.

Models of good practice. In an attempt to influence the local authority, campaign organisations with which we have been linked have cited examples of 'positive' policy initiatives already being undertaken in other parts of the country, in order to build up a case for local change. The purpose of referring to models of good practice has been to convince sceptics that local demands are being implemented elsewhere and thus are respectable.

In Wolverhampton evidence was collected from a number of other local authorities where attempts had been made to develop youth policies which were considered more responsive to the needs of local groups. In 1981, for instance two of the authors carried out an investigation into Inner London Education Authority's (ILEA) Youth Service which was subsequently drawn up as a report and submitted to the local authority's branch committee for consideration (Gabriel and Stredder, 1981). Although ILEA's youth service in reality suffered from many of the criticisms levelled in general at youth service provision, for example it existed within the same legal constraints as other local youth services, it had departed in a number of ways from conventional local authority wisdom. It had its own philosophy, which made explicit its commitment to the participation of young people in planning youth provision, and it also sought to integrate and coordinate policy responses to young people across a wide range of public service provision. Finally it made an explicit commitment to combat racism. In seeking to implement these principles, ILEA had developed not only its orthodox youth club-based provision but also self-help project work detached from youth club premises, which a number of ILEA officers argued was a more sensitive way of meeting the needs of a wider range of groups within the community. Even in the case of youth club provision the authority was developing a more flexible approach, going some way towards meeting the counselling needs and changes in employment and other social conditions which had affected young black people in particular. Finally the representation of black people within the youth service with experience of youth club members and part-time leaders was certainly considerably higher than in Wolverhampton at the time.

Each of these points of contrast was thus debated in turn at one of the branch committee meetings. What many officers and politicians regarded as impracticable were shown to have worked elsewhere and what many officers regarded as extreme demands were shown to be written into the philosophy and practice of London's youth service.

Although officers and politicians appeared receptive at the time to the weight of evidence from ILEA, from the NYB and the NAYC, and the reports of the CRE and the Thompson Committee, they were nevertheless in a position if they so wished, to ignore it, which until 1984, seven years after the first WCCR/CRE report, was more or less what they did. The limited concessions they did make on the appointment of four full-time youth leaders of Afro-Caribbean and Asian descent and the establishment of a three year research project to review youth provision in the town hardly added up to a radical restructuring of local youth policy. Although central initiatives have played some role in securing those concessions, the absence of any legislative backing, combined with the dearth of local commitment has resulted in a minimal response by the local authority. Without the local authority's support, local organisations and groups have thus failed to turn a framework of central initiatives, which although fragmented, are nevertheless favourably disposed to change, into local reality.

Local struggles for educational change in Wolverhampton

Throughout the period of our research project and for nearly a decade before that, a wide range of local organisations were actively involved in campaigning for educational reforms aimed at redressing racial inequalities. In some cases these campaigns centred around particular incidents, that is *individual* cases of injustice and discrimination. The turban case, for instance referred to above (p. 105) falls into this category. More commonly however campaigns have taken a much lower public profile, challenging deficiencies in *institutional* provision and practice. Our intention in this chapter is not to focus on these local campaigns as such but rather on a variety of central initiatives which have proved significant in the development of local struggles.

Legislation   Despite their flaws and weaknesses, both the Race Relations Act (1976) and Section 11 of the 1966 Local Government Act have helped to legitimate local struggles for racial equality. They have done so partly through the provision of resources, in the case of the Race Relations Act through the CRE, and with Section 11 through the funding of specialist staff. More importantly both Acts place obligations on local authorities which however loosely formulated and badly administered (see above p. 143) at least have some legal sanction.

We have already made reference to Section 71 of the Race Relations Act in our examination of Liverpool's campaign for an equal opportunity policy. In Wolverhampton the Local Authority produced a policy statement in 1981, declaring its commitment to equal opportunity both in terms of service provisions and delivery. How far this was the direct result of the 1976 Act is difficult to say. It was certainly one of several authorities during the early 1980s, who declared their commitment to equal opportunity following the lead taken by a number of London boroughs. Despite criticisms of this type of policy statement (as the Liverpool experience confirms, the struggle for the policy's introduction has been matched only by the struggle for its implementation) it has, in Wolverhampton's experience, at least helped to shift the balance and consensus of political debate. In education, this has created an almost imperceptible but nonetheless significant, shift in the starting point for discussions about the nature and source of educational problems about policy objectives and/or what is feasible in terms of the development of alternative strategies. What initiatives have thus been taken from the late 1970s, for example in mother tongue teaching, have emerged out of a context, at least one strand of which can be traced back to the 1976 Act.

Despite the significance of Section 11 to Wolverhampton's local expenditure programmes and its connection with race, the provision never established itself as a local issue until 1983/4 when the government issued its circular outlining changes to the arrangements for funding. For eighteen years local organisations had somehow allowed the local authority to claim approximately two million pounds per year without ever seeking to promote local debate on the issue. This was due partly to the fact that the funding was only allowed for the appointment of local authority staff, and partly because the authority treated it largely as central grant aid. Effectively these arrangements excluded Afro-Caribbean and Asian communities. As a result local organisations and groups continued to focus on those issues already highly politicised and capable of attracting certain kinds of local political/community support, such as immigration and policing, rather than seeking to realise the political potential of what had been turned into a series of administrative procedures.

Two factors did eventually turn Section 11 into a local political issue. We have already mentioned the changes in funding arrangements introduced in 1983 which required community consultation. In the case of Wolverhampton, we need to look at these changes in the context of the local elections in 1984. The first application for funding under the new arrangements was made by the local authority without consulting local minority communities. Since consultation was a requirement imposed on local authorities, under the new arrangements, local groups had a legitimate grievance and one which had the support of central government. The issue came to a head, as issues often do, prior to the local election, with the Labour Group committing themselves to consultation and local community organisations not only talking of withdrawing their support from the local Labour Party, but threatening to write to the Home Office encouraging central government to cut Wolverhampton's grant unless the terms of the arrangements were adhered to by the local authority. A letter was ultimately sent and the Labour Group on behalf of the local authority did agree to consultative meetings with WCCR to comply with the new terms. The extent to which WCCR takes advantage of this access to the Labour Group and the extent to which the Labour Group itself fulfills its new obligations remains to be seen. In other words it may become possible to develop new posts within the authority whose briefs fulfil criteria for Section 11 funding. On the other hand the Group may succeed in using the consultative meetings with WCCR in the same way as it has on occasions used the existence of the race relations committee: as proof of consultation whilst policy decisions are taken elsewhere in the authority.

Policy statements/reports The strength of legislation lies in part in its sanctioning powers and also in the resources which it releases for the purposes of enforcement and administration. Committee reports and policy documents lack both of these and this clearly serves to weaken their impact. Nevertheless they can and have been used to provide additional weight to arguments for local reform.

By far the strongest commitment of central government to multi-racial education has been in the area of English language training for immigrants. Two documents are particularly important in this respect, a DES pamphlet *English for Immigrants* (DES, 1965b) and subsequently *The Continuing Needs of Immigrants* (DES, 1972). Not only did the DES commit itself to overcoming the problems resulting from linguistic differences, it took the exceptional step of giving practical and detailed advice on how such educational provision might be made at a local level. Interestingly, the DES has not continued this practice of making detailed proposals available to LEAs despite a continuing pressure from educational lobbies to reconsider priorities in multi-racial educational provision. Many of the local schemes subsequently introduced came from the 1965 pamphlet, for example the use of reception classes made up entirely of immigrant children. Additional staffing for this sort of practice as well as the staff support required for withdrawal classes, peripatetic teaching and the newly established language centres prompted the Government to make funds available.

Perhaps equally strong, at least initially, was a government commitment to dispersal (DES, 1965a). Despite this directive LEAs generally refused to implement its proposals, an argument which is often used nowadays for not issuing directives on multi-racial education. Where it was attempted dispersal proved both disruptive in terms of breaking up local communities and ineffective in terms of increasing achievement levels of racial minorities.

Since these early policies there has been some detectable shift in official thinking on multi-racial education. Initially, in the early 1970s this took the form of a somewhat half-hearted commitment to some sort of curriculum innovation and at the same time a commitment to tackle the general problems of educational disadvantage regardless of its specific (e.g. racial) dimensions. The ambivalence of the DES over the question of special provision is well illustrated during this period. It is reflected for instance in the significance attached to ethnic custom and language on the one hand (DES, 1971) and its reassurances elsewhere that the curriculum need not be turned upside down and that timetable constraints would necessarily restrict innovation to a minimum (DES, 1974). The late sixties and early seventies thus witnessed a change in the philosophy of multi-racial education but beyond this made little effort to ensure its realisation in practice.

The most recent period from the mid-1970s onwards has witnessed a strengthening of Government commitment to extend the earlier and narrower conception of multiracial education. In the White Paper *The West Indian Community*, for instance, the Government wrote 'in the Education Service we must try to ensure equal opportunity and this will also call for special measures . . . in favour of those with special difficulties' (para 18) and later 'for the curriculum to have meaning and relevance for all pupils now in our schools, its content, emphasis and the values and assumptions contained must reflect the wide range of cultures, histories and lifestyles in our multi-racial society' (Home Office, 1978a, para. 20). This is confirmed elsewhere, for example in the White Paper *Racial Discrimination* (Home Office, 1975, para. 66) and the Green (Discussion) Paper *Education in School* (DES, 1977, para. 10:23). Although there is a tendency in this document to attribute the difficulties to black pupils rather than to the process of schooling there is nevertheless an acknowledgement of broader institutional responsibilities. The White Paper, *Racial Discrimination*, also acknowledges some very specific dimensions of disadvantage, entailing the need to encourage more young people and suitable adults from racial minorities to enter the teaching profession (para. 37) as well as the need to introduce monitoring machinery to teacher education ultimately in order to improve racial minority numbers. Indeed the practice of record keeping, dropped by the DES in 1972, is advocated in this document by the Government as part of a more general attempt to monitor the impact of multi-racial initiatives on school performance (para. 25).

More recently still the reports of the Rampton (Committee of Inquiry, 1981) and the Swann Committee (Education for All, 1985) which looked into the factors affecting different levels of school achievement particularly amongst those of Afro-Caribbean descent, both acknowledged the significance of racial discrimination and the need for schools to adopt clear policies on combating racism. Whatever criticisms might be levelled at the report, including its own particular conception of racism, the making of this single point constituted an advance on previous reports, White Papers etc. This is not to argue that the above documents cannot be flawed, for they all fail to grasp the complexities of institutionalised racism within education. Nevertheless they have proved significant in local struggles if for no other reason than for their acknowledgement of a problem in the face of institutional resistance and indifference. What is more they have increasingly identified that problem in terms of institutional deficiences as well as public responsibilities. Used selectively they have facilitated a more advanced discussion of educational policy within the local authority and, alongside the resource fundings of the Schools Council and National Foundation for Educational Research have helped to legitimate demands for extending provision (Metropolitan Borough of Wolverhampton, 1983).

National organisations: the case of the NUT   The role of the local branch of the National Union of Teachers (Wolverhampton Teachers' Association (WTA)) in developing policy in multi-racial education must be viewed to some extent within the context provided by the NUT's Executive Committee. From 1977 to 1985 this Committee has produced eight pamphlets outlining its response to issues in the area of race and education. The pamphlets represent not only a set of guidelines for practicing teachers but they also outline the position of the NUT in respect of central government's policies on education for racial minority groups. For instance, as well as providing information and advice for teachers on racial stereotyping in textbooks, on mother-tongue teaching, and on the issue of race and intelligence, they also include evidence submitted to the Rampton Committee and comments on the use and replacement of Section 11. In addition to developing its own policy and the implications of this for its local branches and membership, the NUT has been instrumental in promoting research into multi-racial education with the School's Council and other research institutions, and it has also collaborated with the DES to provide in-service training courses for teachers.

Not surprisingly there has been a noticeable shift in the position adopted by the NUT towards the idea of institutional racism, and its relationship to the education system. In the pamphlet *All Our Children*, the Union confirmed its long held belief that teachers could not be, and were not, racists. It did this by reproducing comments submitted to the Home Office in 1968, which state 'Educationists have always claimed with justifiable pride that discrimination (on grounds of colour, race, ethnic or national origin) is not practised at all in the field of education' (NUT, 1978a). Yet in its pamphlet on *Combatting Racialism in Schools*, there is a paragraph on teacher attitudes and expectations which reads: 'No teacher should express racialist views, either through their remarks or conduct; such behaviour would be regarded as unprofessional' (NUT, 1982). In principle therefore, the central organising body of the NUT has finally addressed the fact that teachers themselves may be racist, and that accordingly the Union has a responsibility to acknowledge and take a stand on this.

In practice, however, the political orientation of the national organisation contrasts sharply with the role of local union branches in the formulation of educational policy. Local union branches in our experience have been primarily concerned with negotiating satisfactory conditions of employment for their membership, such as salaries, pension and retirement schemes, staff development, pupil-teacher ratios. The institutional mechanism for the discussion of these issues is the Joint Consultative Committee, which is made up of representatives from all local teacher unions, (the National Union of Teachers, Assistant Masters and Mistresses Association, the National Association of Schoolmasters and National Association of Teachers in Further and Higher Education), education officers, the Chairman of the local authority's education committee and other councillors whose responsibilities include education. The local association of the NUT, the Wolverhampton Teachers' Association, is thus in a relatively privileged position in having this kind of access to officers and members of the LEA by comparison with other kinds of local pressure groups. Despite this privileged access, the JCC has not provided a context for local negotiations and debate on national union policies on race and education.

On one occasion the local association did become directly involved, albeit fleetingly, in an attempt by local organisations to press for local changes in local educational provision. In 1978, at the initiative of the Wolverhampton Anti-Racist Committee (WARC), a series of working parties on multi-racial education were established. WTA were involved through their representation on WCCR. The local Joint Consultative Committee agreed to confer official status on the working parties and agreed to establish a sub-committee to review the reports and make recommendations to the LEA. Ultimately the JCC's main response was to propose the circulation of the working parties' reports to local schools. Despite the scanty and inconclusive nature of the reports, they nevertheless provided WTA with an opportunity to legitimise and prioritise the issue of race and education on the JCC's agenda. This would have ensured the involvement of other local union branches and simultaneously confronted both offices of the LEA and members of the Education Committee with a breadth and strength of opinion which might have been used to develop a detailed and comprehensive local policy.

The failure of the WTA to use the strength of its position to push the JCC on the race issue must be due in part to the failure of the local association to develop a local response to national NUT policy, and to utilise what national resources were available. On the other hand this failure must also reflect on the nature of the framework laid down by the national body. The preoccupation of the local association with issues of pay and conditions and its inability to take up other matters of union policy means that the national organisation has little political effect on its local branches.

Models of good practice   Local authorities in our experience, are extremely adept when it comes to justifying their resistance to local demands for change. Wolverhampton's education department has been no exception in this respect. Invariably recommendations from such groups as the Indian Workers Association, the Pakistani League, the West Midlands Caribbean Association, WARC and WCCR have been rejected on the grounds of their impracticability. This is sometimes linked to the lack of financial resources to pay for them, the lack of staffing resources to implement them or the sheer unreasonableness of the principles underpinning the demands. Examples of 'good practice', or rather practices which constitute at least an advance on Wolverhampton's policy and provision, have thus been used to demonstrate the viability of local demands, at least in the experience of LEAs outside Wolverhampton. In a report on multi-racial education written by two of our research group in 1981 and subsequently adopted by the local constituency Labour Party, four kinds of good practice initiative were identified (Stredder and Gabriel, 1981). The first of these included examination courses which had deliberately been developed or adopted in response to an anti-racist or multi-racial syllabus/curriculum. Afro-Caribbean literature and Asian language were identified as examples, and the innovative use of a variety of exam modes were also discussed. A second category of initiatives defined by the report were the non-examined courses such as lower school humanities. In both of these categories the report highlighted the sorts of changes that had been introduced at the school level in the neighbouring local education authorities of Sandwell and Coventry.

The report also referred to two further aspects of educational policy and provision which illustrated the means by which change could be instituted. Project initiatives, that is initiatives of an experimental nature and with a role as catalyst, were cited as·an important area for development. ILEA's Afro-Caribbean Education Resource Project was used to exemplify this type of initiative. Also, the support services, which traditionally have included English as a second language but now include in-service training and advisory services, were discussed in terms of their potential contribution to reshaping the whole of the 'local curriculum'.

These examples of good practice thus provided the basis for one section of the report on multi-racial education and were brought together with the specific intention of using it in local campaign activity in Wolverhampton. The report was discussed in a number of local Labour Party branches and at a specially convened meeting of the Wolverhampton Teacher Association's Executive Committee. The authority's continued resistance to any radical overhaul of local educational philosophy and practice has meant the kinds of initiatives referred to above remain largely ignored. More characteristically those initiatives which have been taken are organised under the auspices of the Multi-Cultural Education Service and are limited in objective, for example, a course on world religions, and a working party on literature in a multi-racial society. Initiatives emerging from individual schools and colleges are also quite restricted in form for instance the mother-tongue pilot schemes, changes in assembly arrangements, and limited forms of parental involvement (Metropolitan Borough of Wolverhampton, 1982).

In conclusion then local organisations and groups have utilised consciously and unconsciously a variety of central initiatives in order to strengthen their campaign case for changes in local educational provision. Some of these initiatives, those with legal backing and resources, are stronger than others but overall they provide non-directive, discretionary and somewhat tentative forms of support which often prove no match for the opposition. Local authorities in general, and Wolverhampton in particular, have developed their own strategies for countering local pressure of which a number were identified in the first part of this chapter. Once again the onus for utilising central initiatives as levers for local change falls on those organisations and groups who are weakest in terms of the degree of their political access to central and local policy-making processes and who are poorly equipped in terms of their financial and staffing resources to offer a challenge to local authority indifference, inertia, and resistance.

Conclusions

This chapter has explored the relationship between central policy initiatives on race, and local politics. It is quite clearly a complex relationship. By way of conclusion, therefore, we shall identify some of its major dimensions. The most striking characteristic of policy initiatives coming from the centre has been the capacity to attract considerable public attention. The visible character of a series of 'special' measures designed both to control immigration and combat discrimination and deprivation has in our view effectively discouraged an examination of the impact of mainstream public provision on racial equality. This tendency to politicise race at the margins of mainstream policy provision has in turn helped to condition local authority responses which have concentrated on the development of initiatives at the periphery and/or on the surface. Race issues assume a public significance, it appears, only insofar as they can be linked to a range of popular media themes: mugging, 'swamping by alien cultures', cash handouts, demonstrations and marches, and street conflicts. The syndrome of high public profile response at central and local authority levels has in turn helped to encourage the development of certain kinds of anti-racist politics in the community. The preoccupation with combating racism's most visible manifestations through demonstrations and protest guarantees an audience, but it doesn't develop the means by which these injustices can be tackled, nor does it allow the low profile, but equally insidious, forms of institutional racism to be identified and attacked.

A second characteristic of race-related policy is to discharge the actual responsibility for making them work to the local level. This tendency to delegate, or abdicate, responsibility downwards is perpetuated by local authorities who in turn leave it to voluntary organisations to press for positive change. This spiral of irresponsibility originates in the policy frameworks laid down centrally which are sufficiently loose, ambiguous and permissive to provide as much scope for inaction as for action of a positive kind. The lack of any positive response in Liverpool thus put the onus on local voluntary organisations to maximise the scope of provisions contained in the 1976 Race Relations Act. Similarly in Wolverhampton attempts to bring youth policy and provision in line with race relations legislation and the recommendations of the Thompson Report fell to voluntary organisations and groups. In other words those on the margins of mainstream politics are entrusted with the responsibility to convert marginal initiatives into mainstream policies. In contrast to the decentralisation of positive measures there would appear a marked tendency in the opposite direction, to centralise, coordinate and regulate policies like immigration and policing which are both visible and negative in terms of their impact on racial equality.

There is a third tendency prevalent in terms of our experience of local authorities, that is to subvert positive race initiatives. The process of subversion can take place in three ways: by using special resources merely to supplement mainstream expenditure for example Section 11 and Inner City Policy; by subsuming initiatives under the bureaucratic machinery of local government for example Section 11, and finally there is a tendency to convert race issues into individual cases, thus atomising the problem through an individual casework approach to its overall solution. These subversive tendencies on the part of local government effectively encourage the depoliticisation of race and its subordination to the interests of local administrative and bureaucratic survival. Central initiatives thus permit if not actively encourage the operation of these tendencies.

Throughout this book we have emphasised the presence of considerable political resistance to positive action programmes on race across the spectrum of local political parties. We have attributed this in part to the lack of any necessary fit between the principles of positive action and mainstream party political ideologies. This has had the effect in our experience of using central initiatives on race as devices for local party manoeuvering rather than as objects of struggle around which coherent and consistent sets of principles and values are at stake. Local organisations and groups committed to anti-racism are thus engaged in struggles on all fronts. They remain isolated in terms of central policy-making processes, including sometimes access to their own parent/national organisations.

They are also removed from both administrative and political wings of local government. These conditions make their struggle an uphill if not a vertical one, in which the effective penetration of institutional boundaries of mainstream politics and policy provision are the exception rather than the rule. Nevertheless, these efforts in our view remain their only option; to maximise what limited opportunities are available and to minimise the effects of a formidable array of counter-pressures.

7 Conclusions

Studies of race and racism invariably conclude with a set of policy or political recommendations or, more ambitiously, with some predictions relating to the future state of race relation. Neither of these options is a particularly appropriate way to conclude this book. Our research has not been about producing evidence of racial inequalities out of which recommendations might appear a fitting conclusion. Rather, our concern has been to analyse the political context in which recommendations have or have not been implemented. Moreover, since we have stressed the specificity and unpredictability of political struggle throughout the book, there is the additional problem of tailoring recommendations to a particular set of conditions and acknowledging that events may well supersede those recommendations and make them redundant or inappropriate. Instead, our conclusions will pose or imply a series of questions and a framework which we believe are crucial to tackling not only racial inequalities, but other sets of inequalities too. The method of action-research has provided a series of contexts which have provided the basis for a constant reformulation, elaboration and development of research problems and analysis. The continuity of this process is always necessary, given the in-built political objective, the elimination of racial inequality, which is attached to the research exercise.

Our conclusions then are designed not so much to conclude, as to provide openings for further work. The framework can be broken down, quite straightforwardly into three parts. The first is concerned with the identification or construction of a problem; the second questions the political means by which problems are re-inforced, if not created; and the third addresses itself to political attempts to challenge those problems: their source, significance and potential.

The sociological construction of problems

Problem-solving is an extremely unfashionable past-time in social science in Britain in the 1980s. In the field of race it was dismissed in the early 1970s on the grounds that it compromised academic purity by adopting institutional (e.g. policy-makers') definitions of the 'problem'. As a result a number of sociologists rejected the notion of a problem of race and referred to any attempt to do otherwise as 'tinkering' and 'social engineering' (Zubaida, 1970). In so doing, sociology missed a significant opportunity to contribute to other political and policy debates on race, as it did in many other areas of sociological concern.

In advocating closer links with policy related issues we are not suggesting that our definitions or interpretations of problems be borrowed or invoked uncritically from policy-makers. Race problems need not be defined, for instance, in terms of the 'numbers of immigrants' or the 'problems' arising from Afro-Caribbean and Asian culture. On the contrary, from the standpoint of our political perspective, social science should seek to deconstruct the problem of race insofar as it is defined in these terms. The problem of racism and racial inequality, however, remain and if they cannot be solved by means of any simple policy related formula, they can at least be the object of political debate and struggle. The reconstruction of the problem in these terms is linked to our political perspective which in terms of its overall objective seeks to identify and to challenge social injustice and inequality. Both of these terms injustice and inequality, can be defined and elaborated in many different contexts. In this book we have focused on racism as a form of injustice and on racial inequalities, primarily although not exclusively analysed in political terms, which result from it.

For many people the above reference to injustice and inequality will inevitably raise the question of the relationship between the problem of racial inequality and that of class inequality and of capitalism. Put another way it will pose the question of the relationship between the struggle for racial equality and the struggle for socialism. One assumption which has underpinned our work from the outset has been the underdevelopment of socialist politics in a number of important ways. The preoccupation with class inequalities (based on property ownership), the recurrent attempts to subordinate all forms of inequality and injustice to class and the need to challenge the system as a whole rather than any of its interdependent (institutional) parts all tend towards a 'big bang' theory of socialism which offers only simplistic analytical and prescriptive solutions to what in our view are complex problems of definitions and stategy. Sociology, in reproducing these simplistic formulae in its analysis, has ironically bred generations of sceptical and cynical students who reject institutional reform in favour of some wider cataclysm. In doing so, many proceed to spend their working lives resigned to accept these wider structural constraints at the expense of a critical analysis of their own institutional context and its potential for positive reform.

We have sought to challenge the disabling effects of socialist politics, and of sociology insofar as it has reproduced these assumptions and prescriptions in its own analysis. Rather than seeing questions of class struggle and ownership as primary, we have implicitly taken the view that issues such as race provide important space for manoeuvre and advance. Not only do we regard struggle for racial equality as part of the struggle for socialist; we also believe it can be used as a basis for constructing a set of socialist values which would facilitate the struggle on broader fronts. In other words the popularisation of racism has thus ironically provided important space for the popularisation of anti-racism which in turn can help to legitimise the broader struggle for socialism.

The arguments developed above have had important implications for our analysis of the state, which has been defined as a set of public institutions, a set of constraints over the private sphere, and as a site of struggle. The concept of struggle has played a central role in our understanding of processes of change and the development of the state. In order to grasp it more fully we have attempted to analyse the various forces operating within the state each with different powers, defined formally and informally with reference to resources, political access and dominant ideologies.

The focus of our analysis of race and the state has been local for a number of reasons. The first is that local public institutions possess significant powers of control over resources and policy development and these in turn provide an important set of foci for local struggle. The second relates to the strength and level of development of anti-racist movement in Britain which, in the mid 1980s, has proved more effective at a local level in terms of its degree of impact and mobilisation. The contrast between national, and at least some local political climates is clearly a significant factor in this respect. These two factors combine to make local public institutions significant in terms of their degree of openness and amenability and which have thus provided important sites of struggle particularly for local organisations committed to racial equality. Even here, however, at the state's most accessible points a set of centralising and oligarchical features have frustrated efforts to effect positive change. Despite belonging to the 'public' at large, the institutions of the local state are ironically popularly conceived as more inaccessible than private institutions. The struggle for racial equality is thus as much a struggle for democracy and one which seeks to turn the state, both in terms of its image and reality, from an object of control and constraint into a popular instrument of positive change.

The state and racial inequality

Those people who have been involved in working actively for racial equality over the last ten to fifteen years can only be struck by the overall slowness if not imperceptibility of change, the regularity with which similar if not identical policy recommendations or proposals are put forward and the all too familiar recurrence of what seem increasingly to be somewhat dated and clichéd debates and arguments. At the start of our formal collaboration as a research group we were, even then, under no illusions, although our involvement had, prior to 1978, remained by and large outside the formal bureaucratic and political structures of local and central government. Increasingly since 1978 we have found ourselves posing the question of the significance of these local public institutions in reinforcing racial inequalities. Our participatory role in local politics proved a crucial methodological device for testing the local state. What were the various levels on which these reinforcing tendencies were operating? What particular ideologies permeated these levels so as to thwart efforts of redress racial inequalities so persistently and so effectively?

Overall the state has come to represent the site of a struggle between unequal forces in which those of anti-racism have, in a number of ways, been made all too aware of their peripheral or marginal status. The anti-racist forces' proposals, their demands and strategies are dubbed extreme and their organisations dismissed as unrepresentative of local black opinion. Similarly they are consulted on an ad hoc basis for instance in the context of one-off conferences or emergency meetings which are invariably precipitated by street conflicts or the like, and largely at the behest of and on terms laid down by the local party leadership and/or principal officers. Whatever shape or form consultation takes, it rarely provides a context for any meaningful or constructive contribution to political, including policy, deliberation. When concessions are made, as they have been in both Liverpool and Wolverhampton, the danger of isolation remains. The creation of race relations committees, the appointment of specialist officers and the funding of one-off cultural projects, though of potential significance, can at the same time often serve to reinforce anti-racism's marginal status vis a vis mainstream politics and policies.

Behind these marginalising tendencies lie a whole array of ideologies, across the political spectrum, which can be distinguished in terms of their origins and particular forms, but which nevertheless converge in terms of their effects. In 1985 Labour held power in both Liverpool and Wolverhampton. In the case of Liverpool's Militant leadership a formal acknowledgement that racism exists has been combined with a rejection of positive action, which is regarded as divisive and subordinate to the broader struggle against class inequalities. To many, Wolverhampton's political leadership can be located at the other end of Labour's own ideological spectrum. Yet its grudging acceptance of positive action belies a commitment to the primacy of the Labour movement and class related issues which serve to discourage an acknowledgement of the specific forms of racial and gender inequalities. Its failure to demonstrate its commitment beyond a series of as yet somewhat superficial concessions, at least in terms of outcome, make it not dissimilar to its Liverpool counterpart. The ideology of labourism would appear to unite the two wings of the party; in adopting these positions both leaderships are in this respect supported by a view which is prevalent within the professional ideologies of the welfare state, that of universalism, which espouses identical treatment for all regardless of background. In this context positive action and special provision are rejected on the grounds that they advocate what is effectively preferential treatment or discrimination in reverse and thus run counter to the spirit of public welfare provision. Both labourism and universalism are colour-blind ideologies which ultimately refuse to acknowledge the unequal effects of racism and the need to tackle it on its own terms.

Town hall bureaucracies reinforce both the above ideologies in a number of ways. They do so through their defensive response to proposals from 'outside' insofar as these imply or appear to imply criticism of past and present policies and practices. Furthermore their assessment of proposed changes is invariably carried out in terms of the criterion of additional cost rather than in terms of the possibility of redistribution of existing resources and responsibilities. Finally there exists a tendency with local public administration to reinterpret and thereby often emasculate positive initiatives through their accommodation within existing bureaucratic and administrative structures. In other words resistance to change is further strengthened through the combination of conservatism, pragmatism and expedience all of which reinforce those dominant ideologies of labourism and universalism referred to above.

Finally, our discussion of ideologies should not lead us to ignore more overt forms of racism which exist within public institutions at all levels. As far as the higher echelons of local government are concerned these views are rarely made public. What can be said is that in some, although not all instances, the more overtly negative ideologies of race provide the basis on which subsequent rationalisations for inaction, of the kind discussed above, are constructed.

Ideologies in turn are bound up with the process of politics and the institutional contexts in which policies are developed and practised. The political process itself operates at a number of levels. Local policies, which are sometimes written, sometimes not, always embody rules or principles for governing practice. Practice refers to the daily conduct of teachers, housing officers, social workers and other professional and non professional public employees and it can be governed in a number of ways through policy intervention. In our view policies have been a cornerstone in the reproduction of local inequalities. Policies can be distinguished in two ways in this respect: those which effectively discriminate and those which by their absence serve to maintain existing inequalities. The presence of certain policies and the absence of others is clearly reflected in practice. The absence of a policy on racial abuse in schools can and has thus served to sanction overt racism in the classroom and in the playground. Under these circumstances existing policies and practices come to be regarded as the norm, as 'natural', however unwittingly racist they are in terms of their operation or effects. Their 'naturalness' can only be upset or challenged effectively through policy intervention.

Local policies and practices are themselves bound in varying degrees by central and regional policies and other forms of intervention. Laws, policy documents, government circulars, as well as documents and statements produced by national bodies and organisations including political parties, are amongst those we have considered. The question of their significance can be considered in some ways as analogous to the role of local policy and practice. On the one hand the vast bulk of mainstream central policy has yet to formally acknowledge racial equality and the need for specific kinds of policy response. Their absence not only serves to sanction many discriminatory practices which hide under the guise of professional discretion. They also serve to condone or legitimate the absence of policies developed at a local level. On the other hand where 'special' policies and laws exist, they are either positively harmful in terms of their effects, like laws and policies on immigration, or they are both marginal and permissive, like race relations legislation and provide only minimal support in local struggles for racial equality.

This book has sought to identify the various ways in which the state has failed to promote policies, both centrally and locally, which challenge institutionalised racism and its resulting inequalities. The significance of these policies has been considered in the context of ideologies whose potency in the case of race has served to rationalise what exists and ultimately to resist attempts to promote positive change. The identification of these ideologies, which we have argued are fragmentary and diverse in origin, and the various levels at which those ideologies obtain a significance, has been established through our own involvement in local politics. We have witnessed at first hand over many years and in numerous contexts the workings of these political structures in the ways discussed and analysed. As members of local organisations we have repeatedly tested those structures. Our knowledge of them in turn has provided an important basis for the development of organisational pressure from below.

Local organisations, research and positive change

The previous section posed questions on what admittedly for us has been one side of an imbalanced equation. The one side represents those forces within formal political structures which serve to reinforce, if not to generate, by implication or default, racial inequalities. On the other side, however, are those forces engaged in struggles for positive change, aiming at challenging racism and redressing racial inequalities. This side of the equation begs its own questions. What role have these forces played in policy development, given the significance we have attached to policy? We need to assess this role in terms of attempts to challenge the political process at its significant points and the extent to which local forces utilise central and local initiatives, turning them to positive advantage. Struggles within the context of the state can and do provide openings for local voluntary organisations, community groups, trade unions and professionals. Policy outcomes or the concrete reforms which result from the struggles can be used both in terms of a strategic assessment of local organisations as well as levers or instruments for further change.

Local voluntary organisations are significant in this process of struggle around 'problems' and policies, if for no other reason than they are in our experience the principal collective means by which the local struggle for racial equality has been pursued. Organisations themselves differ in terms of their more specific and immediate objectives, their strategies and their relationship to formal political structures. In terms of this framework, anti-racist and community organisations can each be distinguished in terms of its approach to the problem of racial inequality and both types of organisation can be distinguished from a third type which has concentrated its efforts on campaigning for policy change via political mobilisation, the building of alliances, lobbying, research, etc. Although we have worked in all three types of organisation, as a group we have concentrated our efforts in the last of these since this has offered the most potential, in our view, for effecting policy and political change. It has been in the context of this kind of organisation, the two Community Relations Councils, and, in Wolverhampton, the local Labour Party, that we have been involved in campaign and pressure group activity in the fields of equal opportunity, housing, education and youth provision. Overall, however the significance of all three kinds of organisations cannot be underestimated.

They represent, in our experience, the principal means by which the struggle for racial equality is pursued. Against these pockets of positive intervention there is a backdrop of indifference and sometimes hostility and contempt for the issue of racial inequality, including, it must be acknowledged, within the Labour Party. The forces of marginalisation thus affect organisations as much as policies and the struggle against pseudo-forms of consultation, charges of extremism and fanaticism, etc., is indeed formidable.

In addition to these external constraints, local organisations are not without their own internal problems and limitations. A part of our research work has been aimed specifically towards local organisations themselves with a view to enhancing their potential for effective intervention. One such problem which local organisations confront, however much they might wish to conceal it or deny it, is their relationship to those local communities or constituencies which they claim to represent. In order to understand this problem it is important to acknowledge the significance of political culture, the strands of which to a lesser or greater extent can be detected in all organisations with which we have had links and which can only be described as exclusive and alienating in terms of its effects.

It is a culture which centres around evening or sometimes weekend, meetings, agendas, reports, constitutions and rules, and budgets. Its long serving participants survive because in common with other cultural traditions, organisational activity becomes a way of life with a social life integrally bound up with political involvement. For the vast majority of the public, however, incorporation within this culture is inconceivable: it involves learning a new language, in some cases developing new aptitudes, such as speaking in public and conforming to a new set of expectations and demands. Moreover, for those whose lifestyles are relatively private, political activity appears unlikely to bring any direct benefits, nor does it appear to be appealing to any higher sense of morality to which they might claim some affinity.

Political organisations thus face something of a dilemma. In order to survive they appear to need to maintain those very traditions which prevent them from developing broader and more direct links with those they claim to represent. Given the significance attached to the issues of representation, community access and democratisation within both Labour parties and CRCs, however, there exists an unambiguous responsibility to develop alternative structures around which needs and interests might be more directly and continuously articulated. In this process it may be as important to decentralise power towards already existing community structures around which popular interest and support is well established as it is to seek to open up existing political structures, which at present only appeal to a minority, to local communities. This may provide greater opportunities for the development of popular public control of the local state.

The politicisation of race by local organisations needs then to include attempts to extend the process of participation and accountability far beyond the confines of the minority of committed members of the organisations themselves to reach out far more widely and deeply into the ethnic minority and the ethnic majority communities alike. This suggestion, however, has often resisted by the British left who fear the prevalence and deep-rootedness of racism in the wider community. Numerous studies have, after all, revealed ominous findings in this respect. In a recent study of political attitudes of young people, Billig and Cochrane (1984) found that over half their sample had views which coincide with those of extreme right wing organisations. More generally in a recent survey of social attitudes 35 per cent admitted to being racially prejudiced and over half said that they would object if a close relative married an Afro-Caribbean or an Asian person. This figure in itself suggests that the first figure of 35 per cent if anything underestimates the extent of popular prejudice. Whether or not we might seek to deny public access to those whose opinions themselves undermine democracy would only constitute part of an answer to this question. The broader reality remains that such opinion whether we seek to deny its expression or not, has already found institutional expression including as we know formal political institutional contexts. Since racial inequalities are perpetuated at all levels including the day-to-day practices of administrators, managers and shop floor employees then these are bound to continue regardless of changes from above, or even certain forms of pressure from below.

Throughout this book we have focused our analysis around local struggles for racial equality. We have looked at these struggles in terms of their relationship to a number of significant political conditions operating locally and centrally as well as more specifically in terms of the local organisations within which struggle has been pursued. Our experiences have been consistently analysed in terms of a formidable set of constraints on the one hand matched against a considerably weaker yet nonetheless significant set of anti-racist forces. The actual significance of the latter is not easy to measure. To the limited tangible political gains must be added the losses which might have been incurred in the absence of anti-racist pressure. The institutionalisation of anti-racism may be some way off but this should not lead us to underestimate or dismiss it as an object of political practice. For those committed to racial equality, including those engaged in research, the broad range of political interventions of the kind analysed in this book are their only viable option.

Bibliography

Anwar, M. (1980) *Voters and Policies: ethnic minorities and the general election 1979* (Commission for Racial Equality).

Barker, M. (1981) *The New Racism* (Junction Books).

Ben-Tovim, G. S. (ed.) (1983) *Equal Opportunities and the Employment of Black People and Ethnic Minorities on Merseyside* (Merseyside Association for Racial Equality in Employment/ Merseyside Area Profile Group, Department of Sociology, University of Liverpool).

Ben-Tovim, G. S., Brown, V., Clay, D., Law, I., Loy, L., Torkington, P. (1980) *Racial Disadvantage in Liverpool – An Area Profile* (Merseyside Area Profile Group, Department of Sociology, University of Liverpool); also in House of Commons, (1981a) vol. III.

Ben-Tovim, G. S. and Gabriel J. G. (1979) 'The Politics of Race in Britain 1962–79: a review of the major trends and of the recent literature', *Race Relations Abstracts*, vol. 4, no. 4; also in Husband (1982).

Ben-Tovim, G. S., Gabriel, J. G., Law, I. and Stredder, K. (1981a) 'Race, Left Strategies and the State' in *Politics and Power, No. 3* (Routledge & Kegan Paul)

Ben-Tovim, G. S., Gabriel, J. G., Law, I. and Stredder, K. (1981b) 'The Equal Opportunity Campaign in Liverpool' in J. Cheetham *et al.* (eds), *Social and Community Work in a Multi-Racial Society* (Harper & Row).

Ben-Tovim, G. S., Gabriel, J. G., Law, I. and Stredder, K. (1982a) 'Race, Politics and Campaign Activity: A comparative study in Liverpool and Wolverhampton' in G. Craig, N. Derricourt and M. Loney (eds), *Community Work and the State* (Routledge & Kegan Paul).

Ben-Tovim, G. S., Gabriel, J. G., Law, I., Stredder K. (1982) 'A Political Analysis of Race in the 1980s' in C. Husband, (ed.) *Race in Britain* (Hutchinson).

Billig, M. and Cochrane, R. (1984) 'I'm not National Front myself but . . .' *New Society* (17 May).

177

Black Linx, Newsletter of Merseyside Community Relations Council, 64 Mount Pleasant, Liverpool, L3 5SH.

British Nationality Act 1981 (HMSO).

Brown, C. (1984) *Black and White Britain – the third PSI survey* (PSI/Heinemann).

Centre for Contemporary Cultural Studies (1982) *The Empire Strikes Back: race and racism in 70s Britain* (Hutchinson).

Cherns, A. B. (1979) *Using the Social Sciences* (Routledge & Kegan Paul).

Commission for Racial Equality (1978) *Multi-Racial Britain – the social services response* (CRE and Association of Directors of Social Services).

Commission for Racial Equality (1981) *Youth in Multi Racial Society – the urgent need for new policies – 'The Fire Next Time'*.

Commission for Racial Equality (1983a) *Race and the Media – thirty years misunderstanding*.

Commission for Racial Equality (1983b) *Code of Practice – Race Relations*.

Commission for Racial Equality (1984a) *Unigate Dairies Limited – a study of recruitment practices* (report of a formal investigation).

Commission for Racial Equality (1984b) *Race and Housing in Liverpool – a Research Report*.

Commission for Racial Equality (1984c) *Annual Report 1983*.

Commission for Racial Equality (1984d) *Racial Equality and the Youth Training Scheme*.

Commission for Racial Equality (1985) *Immigration Control Procedures – report of a formal investigation*.

Committee of Inquiry into the Education of Children from Ethnic Minority Groups Interim Report (1981) *West Indian Children in Our Schools*, (Cmnd 8273, HMSO).

Commonwealth Immigrants Act 1962 (HMSO).

Commonwealth Immigrants Act 1968 (HMSO).

Daniel, W. (1968) *Racial Discrimination in England* (Penguin Special).

Department of Education and Science (1965a) *The Education of Immigrants. Circular 7/65* (HMSO).

Department of Education and Science (1965b) *English for Immigrants* (Ministry of Education Pamphlet No. 45, HMSO).

Department of Education and Science (1971) *The Education of Immigrants: education survey 13* (HMSO).

Department of Education and Science (1972) *The Continuing Needs of Immigrants: education survey 14* (HMSO).

Department of Education and Science (1974) *Educational Disad-*

vantage and the Educational Needs of Immigrant Children
(Cmnd 5720, HMSO).

Department of Education and Science (1977) *Education in Schools – a consultative document* (HMSO).

Department of Education and Science (1982) *Experience and Participation – a report of the review group on the youth service in England* (Cmnd 8686, HMSO).

Department of the Environment (1977a) *Inner Areas Studies: Liverpool, Birmingham and Lambeth; summaries of consultants' final reports* (HMSO).

Department of the Environment (1977b) *Policy for the Inner Cities* (Cmnd 6845, HMSO).

Edgar, D. (1977) 'Racism, Fascism and the Politics of the National Front', *Race and Class* vol. XIX, no. 2.

Education A weekly journal of the Association of Education Committees, concerned with education administration, management and policy. Longman Group, The Pinnacles, Fourth Avenue, Harlow, Essex.

Education for All: The Report of the committee into the Education of Children from Ethnic Minority Groups. Lord Swann, Chairman (1985) (Cmnd 9452, HMSO).

Edwards, J. and Batley, R. (1978) *The Politics of Positive Discrimination: an evaluation of the Urban Programme 1967–77* (Tavistock).

Employment Gazette, official journal of the Department of Employment, Caxton House, Tothill Street, London SW1 H9NF.

Fitzgerald, M. (1984) *Political Parties and Black People* (Runnymede Trust).

Fryer, P. (1984) *Staying Power – the history of black people in Britain* (Pluto Press).

Gabriel, J. G. and Stredder, K., (1982) *The Youth Service and Provision for Racial Minorities – the case of ILEA* (unpublished paper).

Gordon, P. (1983) *White Law – racism in the police, courts and prisons* (Pluto Press).

Gordon, P. and Klug, F. (1984) *Racism and Discrimination in Britain – a select bibliography 1970 – 1983* (Runnymede Trust).

Hall, S. (1981) 'The Whites of their Eyes – racist ideologies and the media' in Bridges, G. and Brunt, R. (eds), *Silver Linings* (Lawrence & Wishart).

Hall, S. *et al.*, (1978) *Policing the Crisis – mugging, the state, and law and order* (Macmillan).

Home Office (1965) *Immigration from the Commonwealth* (Cmnd 2739, HMSO).

Home Office (1967) *Guidelines on Section II* (Circular 15/1967).

Home Office (1975) *Racial Discrimination* (Cmnd 6234, HMSO).

Home Office (1978a) *The West Indian Community* (Cmnd 7186, HMSO).

Home Office (1978b) *Proposals for Replacing Section II of the Local Government Act 1966* (HMSO).

Home Office (1981) *Racial attacks – report of a Home Office Study* (HMSO).

Home Office (1982) *Revised Guidelines on Section 11* (Circular 97/1982).

Home Office (1983) *Further Revised Guidelines on Section 11* (Circular 94/1983).

House of Commons Home Affairs Committee (1981a) *Racial Disadvantage Vols 1–3* (HMSO).

House of Commons Home Affairs Committee (1981b) *Commission for Racial Equality Vols 1–2* (HMSO).

House of Commons Select Committee on Race Relations and Immigration (1973) *Education Vols 1–3* (HMSO).

Husband, C. (ed.) (1982) *'Race' in Britain – continuity and change* (Hutchinson).

Immigration Act 1971 (HMSO).

Inner Urban Areas Act 1978 (HMSO).

Kettle, M. and Hodges, L. (1982) *Uprising: the police, the people and the riots in Britain's cities* (Pan).

Labour Party Race Relations Action Group (1978) *Racial Equality – the role of local authorities*.

Labour Party Race Relations Action Group (1979) *Local Authorities: ethnic record-keeping and monitoring*.

Law, I. G. and Henfrey, J. (1981) *A History of Race and Racism in Liverpool 1660–1950* (Merseyside Community Relations Council).

Lees, R. and Smith, G. (1975) *Action Research in Community Development* (Routledge & Kegan Paul).

Little, A. and Willey, R. (1981) *Multi-Ethnic Education – the way forward* (Schools Council Working Paper no. 18).

Liverpool City Council, Minutes of Policy and Finance Committee and Race Relations Liaison Committee.

Local Government Act 1966 (HMSO)

Local Government Grants (Ethnic Groups) Bill, House of Commons, 1979 (HMSO).

Manchester Law Centre (undated) *The Thin End of the White Wedge – the new nationality laws*.

Merseyside Anti-Racialist Alliance (1979) *Merseyside Against Racism – first annual report* (MARA).

Metropolitan Borough of Wolverhampton (1983) *Multi-Cultural Education – Report of the Director of Education*.

National Union of Teachers (1978a) *All Our Children*.

National Union of Teachers (1978b) *Section 11 – An NUT Report*

National Union of Teachers (1980) *The Achievement of West Indian Pupils*.

National Union of Teachers (1982) *Combatting Racialism in Schools*.

National Youth Bureau (1981) *Young and Black in Britain*.

Ohri, A., Manning, B. and Curno, P. (eds), (1982) *Community Work and Racism* (Routledge & Kegan Paul).

Ouseley, H. (1984) 'Local Authority Race Initiatives' in Boddy, M. and Fudge, C. (eds) *Local Socialism?* (Macmillan).

Ouseley, H. *et al.* (1982) *The System* (Runnymede Trust/South London Equal Rights Consultancy).

Police and Criminal Evidence Act 1984 (HMSO).

Policy Studies Institute (1983) *Police and People in London*.

Prashar, U. (1984) 'The Need for Positive Action' in J. Benyon (ed.), *Scarman and After* (Pergamon Press).

Race and Immigration: the Runnymede Trust Bulletin, published monthly by the Runnymede Trust, 37a Gray's Inn Road, London WC1 8PS.

Race Relations Act 1965 (HMSO).

Race Relations Act 1968 (HMSO).

Race Relations Act 1976 (HMSO).

Rose, E. J. B. *et al.* (1969) *Colour and Citizenship – a report on British race relations* (Institute of Race Relations/Oxford University Press).

Runnymede Trust (1984) *Deportations and Removals*.

Scarman, Lord (1981) *The Brixton Disorders April 10th–12th, 1981: a report of an inquiry* (Cmnd 8427, HMSO).

Sivanandan, A. (1982) *A Different Hunger – writings on black resistance* (Pluto Press).

Smith, D. J. (1977) *Racial Disadvantage in Britain* (Penguin).

Stredder, K. and Gabriel, J. (1981) 'Multiracial Education in Wolverhampton – the case for local reform' (unpublished paper).

Tomlinson, S. (1983) *Ethnic Minorities in British Schools – a review of the literature 1960–82* (PSI/Heinemann).

Townsend, H. E. R. and Brittan, E. (1972) *Organisation in Multi-Racial Schools* (NFER).

Wolverhampton Anti-Racist Committee (1978) *Support the Wolverhampton Anti-Racists – drop all the charges!* (WARC).

Wolverhampton Council for Community Relations (1977) *Youth Provision in Wolverhampton* (WCCR/CRE).

Wolverhampton Council for Community Relations (1984) Submission to Youth Review, Wolverhampton Borough Council.

Wolverhampton Southwest Labour Party Race Relations Policy Group (1981) *Report on Youth Provision in the Borough of Wolverhampton with particular reference to Racial Minorities.*

Wolverhampton Southwest Labour Party Race Relations Policy Group (1982) *Education Provision in a Multiracial Society – Proposals for Local Reform.*

Young, K. and Connelly, N. (1981) *Policy and Practice in the Multi-Racial City* (Policy Studies Institute).

Zubaida, S. (ed.) (1970) *Race and Racialism* (Tavistock).

Index

183